ORCHIDS

The Complete Grower's Guide

ORCHIDS
The Complete Grower's Guide

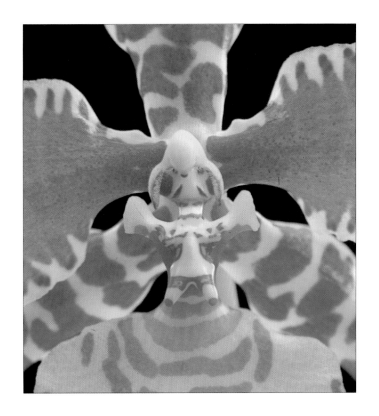

Wilma and Brian Rittershausen

with special photography
by Derek Cranch

GARDEN•ART•PRESS

First published 2001
©2001 Wilma and Brian Rittershausen
World copyright reserved

ISBN 1 870673 34 4

British Library Cataloguing-in-Publication Data
A catalogue record for this book is available from the British Library

Frontispiece: *Cymbidium* Bulbarrow 'Friar Tuck' AM/RHS
Title page: *Rossioglossum* Rawdon Jester

Origination by Garden Art Press, a division of Antique Collectors' Club
Woodbridge, England
Printed and bound in Italy

Antique Collectors' Club

The Antique Collectors' Club was formed in 1966 and quickly grew to a five figure membership spread throughout the world. It publishes the only independently run monthly antiques magazine, *Antique Collecting*, which caters for those collectors who are interested in widening their knowledge of antiques, both by greater awareness of quality and by discussion of the factors which influence the price that is likely to be asked. The Antique Collectors' Club pioneered the provision of information on prices for collectors and the magazine still leads in the provision of detailed articles on a variety of subjects.

It was in response to the enormous demand for information on 'what to pay' that the price guide series was introduced in 1968 with the first edition of *The Price Guide to Antique Furniture* (completely revised 1978 and 1989), a book which broke new ground by illustrating the more common types of antique furniture, the sort that collectors could buy in shops and at auctions rather than the rare museum pieces which had previously been used (and still to a large extent are used) to make up the limited amount of illustrations in books published by commercial publishers. Many other price guides have followed, all copiously illustrated, and greatly appreciated by collectors for the valuable information they contain, quite apart from prices. The Price Guide Series heralded the publication of many standard works of reference on art and antiques. *The Dictionary of British Art* (now in six volumes), *The Pictorial Dictionary of British 19th Century Furniture Design, Oak Furniture* and *Early English Clocks* were followed by many deeply researched reference works such as *The Directory of Gold and Silversmiths,* providing new information. Many of these books are now accepted as the standard work of reference on their subject.

The Antique Collectors' Club has widened its list to include books on gardens and architecture. All the Club's publications are available through bookshops world wide and a full catalogue of all these titles is available free of charge from the addresses below.

Club membership, open to all collectors, costs little. Members receive free of charge *Antique Collecting*, the Club's magazine (published ten times a year), which contains well-illustrated articles dealing with the practical aspects of collecting not normally dealt with by magazines. Prices, features of value, investment potential, fakes and forgeries are all given prominence in the magazine.

Among other facilities available to members are private buying and selling facilities and the opportunity to meet other collectors at their local antique collectors' clubs. There are over eighty in Britain and more than a dozen overseas. Members may also buy the Club's publications at special pre-publication prices.

As its motto implies, the Club is an organisation designed to help collectors get the most out of their hobby: it is informal and friendly and gives enormous enjoyment to all concerned.

For Collectors — By Collectors — About Collecting

ANTIQUE COLLECTORS' CLUB
5 Church Street, Woodbridge, Suffolk IP12 1DS, UK
Tel: 01394 385501 Fax: 01394 384434
Email: sales@antique-acc.com Website: www.antique-acc.com
or
Market Street Industrial Park, Wappingers' Falls, NY 12590, USA
Tel: 845 297 0003 Fax: 845 297 0068
Email: info@antiquecc.com Website: www.antiquecc.com

Photographic Credits

The authors wish to thank the following contributors for the use of their photographs which are reproduced in this book:

Dr. Henry Oakeley, Chairman of RHS Orchid Committee
Photographs 1, 2, 3, 5, 6, 7, 8, 9, 10, 11, 12

H. Zakharoff
Photograph 4

Ian Plested, Chairman of the British Orchid Growers' Association
Photographs 13, 14, 15, 16

Ned Nash, Director of Conservation, the American Orchid Society
Photographs 17, 18, 19, 20, 21, 22, 23, 24, 25, 26

Dr. Peter Sander, great grandson of Frederick Sander, founder of Sander of St. Albans
Photograph 29

Contents

Preface

Orchids are enjoying a popularity that could not have been dreamed of, even in the heyday of the Victorian 'orchid mania'. No longer the exclusive preserve of the aristocracy, the wealthy industrialists, the manufacturers of mustard or the owners of banks, the last years of the second millennium and the dawn of the third have witnessed this astonishing, almost unsung, renaissance in orchid growing. Changes in cultivation practices with computerised and mechanised greenhouses, vast laboratories cloning the latest orchids day and night, and the age of international transport have made orchids the most popular pot-plant in Europe and available to the world. Greenhouses in Holland produce up to two million orchids as pot plants per acre per year and with insatiable demand in Japan and the USA, the global production of orchids for commerce passed the billion a year mark some time ago. Orchid shows in Japan see crowds of up to 75,000 people per day – and nearly half a million in nine days – and everywhere we see orchids being grown in houses and gardens, where their elegance and longevity provide pleasure for us all.

The amateur specialist growers, with greenhouses, still enjoy the delights of the exotic species, the esoteric thrill of looking at exquisite flowers of miniscule orchids such as *Lepanthes*, with the aid of a hand lens. For those of us, however, who enjoy the perfection in our flowers without the need to know Latin names, the orchid hybrids that have been bred for ease of cultivation in the house and garden are all we need. One only has to have an elegant *Phalaenopsis* – the Moth Orchid – in flower at home for months on end, to be permanently captivated by these entrancing plants. Little could Darwin have realised that the same characteristics of the flowers that developed in orchids to attract insect pollinators, are now being used by hybridisers to attract humans. In the wild, orchids which are successful in attracting pollinators survive and prosper; growing on rocks, trees, cacti, even as subterranean plants and wherever they can find a niche. Now, orchids which are successful in attracting hybridisers are colonising the world's window-sills and sitting-room tables, finding these new habitats as the forests and wild places of the world disappear, so ensuring the survival of their ancient gene pool and their magical beauty.

Brian and Wilma Rittershausen have been central figures in amateur orchid growing in Britain for half a century, and Burnham Nurseries founded by their father in 1949 has been the happy hunting ground for several generations of enthusiasts. In this book they introduce us to the different orchid genera that are popular today, with beautiful photographs and their easy prose. This book will be an inspiration to many to grow and enjoy the rich selection of orchids that are now available.

Dr. Henry Oakeley
Chairman, Orchid Committee of the Royal Horticultural Society
President, Orchid Society of Great Britain

Foreword

In the first five chapters of this book we cover the most desirable aspects of orchids from getting to know the plants and understanding how they grow in their natural environments, the discovery of the tropical epiphytes, their first importations and subsequent exploitation, to today's mass-marketing in a global world. We progress through all cultural techniques with clear step-by-step illustrations to show the various repotting procedures and all other aspects of their culture. By far the largest chapter is reserved for the orchids themselves, and in the last chapter we deal exclusively with a varied range of orchids you can grow in a greenhouse or the home.

From the many thousands of species and hybrids which exist, we have selected those which attract the greatest admiration, or are renowned for having the most pleasing qualities of showy blooms, longevity, and ease of flowering under cultivation by an amateur. We have therefore grouped our selection in order of popularity, starting with the best-loved and well-known genera, with the emphasis, wherever possible, on the modern hybrids which are readily available today.

Where little or no hybridising has been done, and species still dominate, or contribute more to a genus, as with the bulbophyllums or coelogynes, these are concentrated upon and given as much prominence as the hybrids.

Further into our selection we detail those less familiar orchids which anyone looking to extend their collection may find singularly attactive in their own way. Even the more obscure and strangely-flowered genera are given space here, for all of them, large and small, weird and wonderful, have their following, and all the plants we mention can be found in cultivation. Many can be seen, along with very many more, at the popular orchid shows which are held at regular venues throughout the year. If you allow them, orchids will take you on a voyage of discovery, one which should not be hurried, or rushed through, but taken at leisure, allowing time to absorb and delight in every new orchid you encounter. In this way, what appears at first to be a bewildering disarray of endless colours and shapes, will gradually focus to reveal similar characteristics which can be seen to follow a designated pattern.

We hope you enjoy your excursion through orchids. It is a very long journey, and one without end.

Wilma and Brian Rittershausen

Chapter One

Getting to Know Orchids

Of all the plant families within the vegetable kingdom it is the orchid which has aspired to the highest point of sophistication. So great are the differences between them, that you could take any random selection and ask, 'How can all these belong to one family?' This diversity has occurred over millions of years of evolution because of the orchid's unique ability to adapt to almost every environment. This has allowed orchids to exist in tropical rain forests as well as arctic regions and to be at home in dry deserts and swamps, woodlands and meadows. They are found from sea level to mountainous plateaux. Extreme temperatures and elevations are no barriers, orchids are among some of the toughest living plants on earth.

While orchids were evolving and spreading throughout the world, they diversified into the highly specialised plants we know today. One important divergent occurred in the

---

1 (Opposite). *Gongora* species growing wild in the jungles of Ecuador. Note the heavy lichen which covers the trees and orchid foliage. In these dense conditions other epiphytes are growing and strong sunlight breaks through the branches of the overhanging canopy.   Photograph: H.F. Oakley

2 (Above). *Lycaste locusta* growing in full sun on rocks, surrounded by thick foliage. This habitat near Mendoza, Peru, obviously suits the plant well, as it is blooming freely.   Photograph: H.F. Oakley

3. *Cycnoches* species from Guatemala growing on a tree stump in a mangrove swamp a metre above water level at Lake Izabal. Note the mass of aerial roots around the base of the plant.   Photograph: H.F. Oakley

4. *Lycaste tricolor* var. *alba* growing epiphytically in Costa Rica on a comparatively young tree where the orchid is safe for many years. The pseudobulbs are shrivelled after enduring a period of dryness. The new growth with masses of flowers came after the rains.
                    Photograph: H. Zakharoff

tropical regions where the extremes of summer and winter are not defined as in temperate areas. Here the seasons alternate from wet and dry, while the temperatures remain on the warmer side. Under these conditions, orchids adapted to an airborne way of life, and became epiphytic, growing on branches and trunks of the forest trees. In this way they could gain access to a fresher, lighter and airier environment in the tree canopy, away from competition of other vegetation on the ground. However, they had to make some adaptations to survive without soil, and they did this by producing pseudobulbs, plump water-storing vessels, to enable them to withstand periods of drought. During these times the mostly evergreen orchids become dormant, which we call resting, relying upon the water stored until the rains returned. Water is taken up by their fleshy aerial roots, which either cling firmly to the tree bark to hold them in place, or trail freely through the air to absorb water and nutrients which sustain the plant. Everything about these epiphytic orchids is designed for a tree-dwelling existence. Their leaves have adapted to receive dappled shade while the trees to which they cling are in leaf, and their flowers are produced in such a way as to be easily seen by passing pollinators. This attraction can be scent or movement, and many epiphytic orchids produce long slender flowering spikes which terminate in a shower of blooms (*Oncidium flexuosum*), needing only the slightest breeze to flutter and dance in full view of the pollinator. Most often these pollinators are insects, but occasionally small flying mammals or birds are attracted by either bright colours or movement which hold the promise of nectar. Although not always given, it is always anticipated.

Orchids growing in the temperate regions of the world retain a terrestrial existence, growing conventionally in the soil. They produce fleshy underground tubers or fibrous roots and mostly have seasonal growth which dies down after flowering, unlike the epiphytes which are mainly evergreen. The terrestrial orchids have a lesser commercial importance than the epiphytes which have captivated men and women with their exotic beauty for thousands of years.

Orchids do not have any permanent parts. The pseudobulbs of the epiphytes are the longest living structures, and these will live for several years before being replaced by younger ones. They are extremely varied in their shape and size and may be from a few millimetres high on the smallest bulbophyllums to 4m on the huge grammatophyllums. They may be squat, rounded, oval or elongated depending on the genus. The pseudobulbs support the leaves, which again differ from each other in shape and size, as well as the number to one pseudobulb. The leaves may be soft and plicate, or ribbed along their length. They may be tough, long and thin, or roundly oval. The width of the leaves depends much upon their natural habitat, plants exposed to much sun have modified and rounded their leaves to resemble a pencil. Some are thick and fleshy living for several years, while others are paper thin, designed to last for one season only.

Orchid roots are mostly thick and fleshy, but may also be much finer. They grow from

5 (Below left). *Oerstedella* species growing on a tree in Costa Rica, in full sunlight together with other epiphytic plants including bromeliads. Photograph: H.F. Oakley

6 (Below right). *Laelia anceps* growing at a high altitude in Mexico. Note the dryness of the tree bark as it has not rained for some time. The plant is thriving and flowering well. All the old pseudobulbs show signs of dead flower spikes where the plant has bloomed regularly over the years. Photograph: H.F. Oakley

8 (Above). *Lycaste* species growing on the roadside in Ecuador amongst long grasses and foliage.

Photograph: H.F. Oakley

9 (Above right). *Zygopetalum intermedia* in Peru, growing in deep wet grass surrounded by ferns. The plant itself is hardly visible and only the flower spike grows above the foliage.   Photograph: H.F. Oakley

the base of each new growth and support the developing pseudobulb for as long as the leaves are retained. An aged pseudobulb will lose its leaves and roots in a natural progression while still retaining some nutrients which continue to support the younger, developing pseudobulbs. These older pseudobulbs, known as backbulbs, are often removed from the plant and used to propagate. Under cultivation, orchid roots will penetrate the compost and fill the container, but many will also grow out into the air around them. These roots have an outer covering, called the velamen, which acts as blotting paper and absorbs moisture to prevent the root from dehydrating. The white velamen follows behind the extending root so that just the green growing tip is exposed. When an orchid is resting the green tip ceases to grow and becomes covered over by the velamen. The roots of *Phalaenopsis* are flattened and silvery and will adhere strongly to any surface that they come into contact with. Paphiopedilums have more fibrous roots which are brownish, and covered in small dense hairs.

Epiphytic orchids have two distinct patterns of growth. The majority are sympodial and

7 (Opposite). *Epidendrum leucochilum* in Venezuela at home on an almost bare rock, receiving little shade from a nearby tree. The plant will have rooted into a few cracks in the rock to make use of any moisture.   Photograph: H.F. Oakley

10 (Above left). *Paphiopedilum callosum* var. *sublaeve* growing as a terrestrial in the jungles of Malaysia at Kedah Peak.

11 (Above right). *Lycaste cruenta* is only detectable by its bright golden flowers nestling in the fork of a very large tree in the jungle of Guatemala, near Coban.

12 (Left). *Lycaste skinneri* at home in a split tree showing a series of old pseudobulbs produced over the years. The roots will find their way deep into the heart of the rotting host which is covered in mosses and polypodium ferns. All are safe until the tree dies and falls to the forest floor. Photograph: H.F. Oakley

produce pseudobulbs. The new growth comes from the base and develops into a further pseudobulb. In this way the plant builds up a string of pseudobulbs, each joined by a short rhizome which in cattleyas and bulbophyllums can be clearly seen. When two new growths are produced from one pseudobulb, the plant divides as new strings are started which will eventually produce two separate plants. Cymbidiums are examples of sympodial orchids with pseudobulbs. On these plants the ageing process can be clearly seen with the older pseudobulbs becoming brown, shrivelled and devoid of leaves. Provided the newest pseudobulbs are green and plump, and the leaves are green and healthy, the plant is well balanced and will continue to grow for many years. Some orchids in cultivation can attain great ages, and among the paphiopedilums are early hybrids which are over one hundred years old. The first of these was *Paphiopedilum* Harrisianum, raised in 1869.

Not all the sympodial orchids produce pseudobulbs. Paphiopedilums follow the sympodial pattern, but make leafy growths consisting of a few to several leaves. These are extremely varied according to the species, some are rigid and fleshy, easily snapped with careless handling, while others are strap-like and of various lengths. Some are attractively mottled while others are plain green. All are handsome plants. Paphiopedilums produce their flower spikes from the centre of the latest mature growth. These may be from one to many-flowered, from a few centimetres high (*Paphiopedilum bellatulum*) or as much as a metre long (*Paphiopedilum rothschildianum*).

In most orchids the racemes, or flower spikes as they are called, are produced from the

13. *Paphiopedilum leucochilum* living on limestone rock with little moss and hardly any humus. These very small plants produce extremely large blooms for their size and will survive in the most inhospitable places.

leading, or latest, pseudobulb or growth. In cymbidiums they start at the base, and can be seen, usually in late summer, protruding from one side of the pseudobulb and gradually extending to resemble a pencil. Following a wait of many months or even years, this evidence of flowering is a magic moment! Odontoglossums and the many related genera which will interbreed with this genus, produce their flower spikes from inside the basal leaf on one side of the pseudobulb. Cattleyas and other plants within this alliance develop their flower spikes from the top of the pseudobulb. A sheath forms at the apex which protects the young developing buds. As they grow the buds push through the sheath which splits easily to allow them to exit. Its work done, the sheath withers and dries, often before the flowers open. Sheaths are not always produced however, when the young buds can be observed as they grow.

Dendrobiums develop elongated pseudobulbs called canes, and these are mostly thin but can be shorter and stouter. They are leafed along their entire length as in *Dendrobium nobile* and its hybrids, or leafed on the upper portions as *Dendrobium phalaenopsis* and its hybrids. The *D. nobile* type produce their flowers, mostly in pairs, from a node sited between the leaves. The *D. phalaenopsis* type produce longer racemes with up to a dozen blooms from the upper part of the canes.

The second pattern of growth is monopodial. *Phalaenopsis* and vandas are examples of those orchids which grow from a central point, the leaves being produced from the tip of an extending upright rhizome. The leaves alternate to either side creating a fan-shaped plant. Some vandas can become considerably tall, a mature plant carrying up to a dozen pairs of leaves reaching to a metre or more. The *Phalaenopsis*, on the other hand, are self-regulating and never attain any great size, which makes them far more desirable as house orchids. They produce their roundly oval, fleshy leaves at intervals of one or two a year, while the same number of leaves is shed so that an adult plant will support four to five leaves at any time.

Monopodial orchids produce long, aerial roots which often become a feature of the plants. Their flower spikes appear from the base of a leaf.

Whichever orchids you look at, it soon becomes apparent that they are different from other plants, and their various modes of growth are fascinating and unique. However, it is not until you gaze at their flowers that the unparalleled richness of diversity and beauty can be readily understood. It only takes one look to appreciate that here is a flower which can amaze, delight and fascinate, leaving many to seek out more and more bewildering forms to satisfy an ever-growing desire. To our minds the orchid flower might have been created solely for the pleasure of those of us who so admire them, but of course, the real purpose of these often extraordinarily beautiful flowers is to attract pollinators, and the ways in which the various orchids have evolved to do this is worthy of further study on its own. Probably the most famous tale relating to an orchid and its specific pollinator is one which has been told many times. It concerns Charles Darwin and the discovery of the Comet Orchid, *Angraecum sesquipedale*, in Madagascar in 1822. This monopodial orchid produces several large, star-shaped, icy-white flowers which each have a 30cm long spur at the back of the lip. While at first its function was unknown, because nectar was found at the base, Darwin predicted there must be a night-flying hawk moth with a proboscis the length of the spur to effect pollination.

14 (Above left). *Cymbidium* species, allied to C. *aloifolium*, growing on a cliff-face in Thailand. Unlike the cultivated hybrids, many of the species have stiffened leaves with bi-lobed ends. These plants are known as lithophytes and are neither true epiphytes nor terrestrials.

15 (Above right). *Cymbidium* species in the dry season in Thailand, withstanding the full tropical sun with little or no moisture for many weeks. The plant will survive like this growing and blooming well during the coming rainy season.

Although ridiculed at the time, later such a hawk moth was discovered, and named *Xanthopan morganii praedicta*. For millions of years, the orchid and insect have co-existed together, one dependent upon the other for its survival. Such is this dependency, were the moth to die out in the wild, the *Angraecum* would also become extinct.

All orchid flowers conform to one basis pattern. There are three outer sepals, which resemble the petals, and three inner petals. The third petal is highly modified and called the lip. The lip is formed to provide a landing platform for the pollinating insect. It is often richly decorated to form a 'honey guide' directing the pollinator to exactly the right position on the flower. Protruding from the centre of the bloom is a single, finger-like structure, called the column. This contains both the male and female parts of the flower with the ovaries contained in the stem behind the flower, which carries the unfertilised seed. At the end of the column is the stigmatic surface area. This is a small sticky

16. *Aerangis mystacidii* in full flower. Many of these African species produce long spurs at the back of the blooms which contain nectar with which the flower tempts the pollinating insect.

depression on the underside of the column, above which, at the tip, is the anther with the pollen underneath. In its pollen the orchid differs most from all other plants, for it is held in little waxy parcels, two or more golden yellow pollinia joined by a short thread. These solid pollen masses ensure that, unlike ordinary pollen which is wind-blown, and therefore wasteful, every grain is used.

When an insect of the right size lands on the flower it has to push its way into the centre of the bloom and by doing so dislodges the pollinia which become attached to its body. The insect flies away with the pollinia still attached and as it visits the next flower the pollinia are deposited upon the stigmatic surface. What may appear to be a straightforward procedure is in fact highly complicated, and orchids have evolved numerous ways of attracting just the right insect and repelling others. In Europe, we need look no further than the native Bee Orchids, *Ophrys* spp. for an amazing example of how the orchid deceives the *Euglossa* bees which swarm over the flowers in early summer. The orchid times its flowering to coincide with the emergence of the male bees, a few weeks before the females

17. *Rhynchostylis coelestis* species in Florida far from its native home in India. Perfectly adapted to life on a palm tree, as a garden plant it makes a spectacular show. Its long aerial roots benefit from the high humidity.

18. *Cymbidium aloifolium* blooming freely with no humus around its roots. An Indian epiphyte in a Miami garden.

19. *Laeliocattleya* Angel Love, a hybrid with masses of bloom, brightens up a dark corner of a tropical garden containing non-flowering palms and cycads.

appear. The Bee Orchid is well named, for its lip is uncannily like the body of the female bee, and to the male specimen looking for a mate, the deception is complete. As the male tries to copulate with the orchid flower, the pollen is collected, and carried to the next flower, and deposited by the same means.

Some of the most weird and outlandish methods adopted for pollination occur with the terrestrial orchids native to Australia. The Hammer-head orchid, *Drakaea elastica* sends its pollinator on a wild, helter-skelter ride, devised by a loosely-hinged lip, which slams the wasp into the pollen!

From the African Congo comes the extraordinary *Bulbophyllum purpureorhachis* whose upwardly spiralling spear-like, flattened stem, or rachis, carries two longitudinal rows of tiny purplish flowers with mobile lips, presumably evolved to be attractive to small social insects such as the ants.

Among the Slipper Orchids, which include the paphiopedilums and phragmipediums, the lip has undergone a further modification and become a pouch, or slipper. The pouch attracts insects which alight on the slippery rim and tumble in. Their exit from the pouch is clearly defined by a ladder of hairs which extend upwards

20. *Phalaenopsis schilleriana* on a palm tree at the side of the path makes a surprising encounter in any tropical garden.

21. Terate-leaved vandas and hard-caned dendrobiums will flourish in any tropical garden. Here they are growing in full light where they will bloom almost continuously throughout the year.

22. A large specimen *Vanda* hybrid which has been established on this palm tree for many years. Note how the roots run up and down the trunk, securing the plant against the strongest of tropical storms.

at the back of the pouch. As the insect climbs, it pushes its way out and in doing so removes or delivers pollen onto one of two stigmatic surfaces, which in these orchids are found on either side of the column. The genus *Coryanthes* has taken this idea one step further. Its common name of Bucket Orchid refers to the pouch-like appendage of the lip which actually holds liquid secreted by the flower. Visiting bees find the fleshy rim of the lip irresistible and compete with each other for a place where they can gnaw at the surface. Inevitably a bee falls into the bucket where it has to swim to an opening through which it can just crawl free. In doing so the pollen is carried from one flower to the next.

Orchids pollinated by insects often rely upon scent to attract the right pollinator. Among the bulbophyllums are found several evil-smelling species whose pungent blooms attract flies looking for carrion. This deception is further emphasised when the lip resembles a piece of raw meat, as in *Bulbophyllum graveolens*. A further species, *B. fletcherianum* produces flowers which, clustered together, bear an uncanny resemblance to the open beaks of young birds in the nest. The sweetest scented orchids such as *Oncidium ornithorhynchum*

23 (Opposite). *Ascocenda* hybrids at the centre with epidendrums below and a *Schomburkia* species above, not in flower, growing together in a tropical garden.

25. *Brassavola nodosa* out of flower in its resting season its foliage baked purple by the blazing tropical sun which it endures throughout the dry season.

24. *Encyclia tampensis* hybrid growing on a palm tree with spreading roots fixing the plant to its host.

are those pollinated by nectar- seeking moths. Some of these flowers are fragrant for just a few hours in the day or night when specific moths are on the wing. Many, such as *Brassavola nodosa* and *Angraecum sesquipedale* are fragrant at night. Night-fragrant orchids are usually white, or have large white lips. Bright colours are displayed by many orchids whose highly decorative lips provide the honey guide. This is most evident among the *Miltoniopsis*, where this marking has been further enhanced by hybridisation, and is called a mask. One species with bright red flowers is *Hexisea bidentata* where the lip varies little from the sepals and petals. The brilliant colouring is designed to attract a small humming bird, and this is one of only a few orchids which do not use insects for pollination.

Once an orchid flower has become pollinated the process of fertilisation commences. The flower parts collapse and wither away while the ovary, which is the stem immediately behind the flower, begins to swell. This continues to fatten over a period of several months to form the seed capsule. Once ripe, the capsule splits along longitudinal lines and the seed trickles out to be blown by the wind over a large area.

The individual orchid seeds are extremely small, like grains of fine sawdust. One capsule can contain up to three million, pale brown, white or golden-yellow seeds. In the wild very few of these seeds will germinate and grow. Because the seed is so fine it carries no reserves of food to start its growth, unlike a pea which is a huge green globe by comparison with sufficient reserves to start a shoot. The orchid seed relies upon a mycorrhizal fungus for its development, and can only grow if it lands where the fungus is present. The seed becomes impregnated with the mycorrhiza and the two living organisms form a symbiotic relationship which enables them both to co-exist and grow. Of the millions of seed wafting through a tropical rainforest, most are wasted, but enough survive to ensure the continuation and evolution of the species. Orchids are perennial, and as we have seen can live for very many years, so do not rely solely on seed production for their continued existence in the same way as annual plants.

26. *Aerides odorata* with masses of buds will soon be in flower. This tangled mat of a plant is perfectly at home in the West Indies, far from its native South East Asia.

Even when the orchid seed has formed its partnership and received basis nutrients in the form of sugars from the mycorrhiza, it is unable to produce leaves or roots. Before it can do this, the seed has to go through a first stage of development and it swells into a small green globule or protocorm rather like a miniature pea. This contains the necessary chlorophyll to sustain further development and only then can the tiny embryo plant produce its first leaves and roots. Several years of slow expansion will follow before the plant reaches flowering size, after which it will bloom and continue to grow for many years. The first orchid hunters found plants over two metres across, completely encircling the tree trunks on which they made their home.

In cultivation, seed production is important for hybridisation and conservation. How this was achieved so that all the seeds would have a chance to grow, we shall look at in a further chapter.

Chapter Two
A History

Although orchid species occur all over the world, it is in the tropical regions near the equator, that the greatest variety of epiphytic types are found, and these are undeniably the most beautiful forms that the orchid has aspired to. This abundance of exquisitely flamboyant species was unknown to the western world until about 200 years ago. It was an age of exploration and ships sailed from Britain to discover new worlds on the other side of the oceans.

The first flamboyant orchid to make an impact reached England in 1822. It was described as *Cattleya labiata*, having arrived from Brazil as packing material around other plants sent to William Cattley, a noted horticulturalist of that time. This was the first showy, large-flowered orchid to be seen, and when it flowered, it was a sensation, and created an immediate demand for more of the wonderful plants. The first orchid collectors were dispatched by the rich land-owners and commercial nurserymen to explore uncharted areas of jungle in the New World. It was not long before large consignments of orchid species were being shipped back to England on a regular basis as the intrepid hunters scoured the virgin forests, often being the first Europeans to explore alien territory. Tales of rivalry, greed, hardships and exploitation followed, as areas were systematically stripped of their orchid treasures and the plants carried away to ports to await the ships. Many previously unknown and undescribed orchids suffered and died on these long journeys, or were lost at sea in shipwrecks so that the numbers of plants reaching England alive were at first comparatively small. Upon arrival troubles for the orchids did not end, for those early enthusiasts to orchid culture had little knowledge of where the plants had come from, they knew nothing of their habitats or manner of growing, and were unable to provide orchids with suitable growing conditions. At first it was thought that because the plants had come from the tropics, they needed a hot, steamy atmosphere in which to grow, and that they had little need of light. Unfortunately, nothing could have been further from the truth, for most of the orchids had been collected at high altitude locations, very far from the sea shore and the hot steamy jungles. The orchids preferred the higher mountain slopes, where the air was cool and light filtered down through the tree canopy to the epiphytics growing upon the tree branches. Moisture fell as rain and mists which clung to the mountain tops was quickly

27 (Opposite). *Cattleya labiata*. The first to be discovered and most famous of the *Cattleya* species, and a parent of nearly all hybrids in this family. Now quite scarce in the wild but commonly cultivated by lovers of the genus. This species originates from Brazil.

28. *Cymbidium devonianum* was the first miniature *Cymbidium* to be discovered in the foothills of the Himalayas in 1843. It flowered for the Duke of Devonshire at Chatsworth in Derbyshire and was named after him. This species has proved to be an important parent in modern *Cymbidium* hybridisation.

dispelled by the sun which dried the leaves quickly, leaving orchids refreshed in the buoyant air.

It took some time for all this information to be relayed to those early growers in Britain and eventually the orchids were removed from the dark, dank ferneries of the day, which suited the ferns which were so popular in Victorian England but not the orchids, and placed in specially constructed glasshouses, which were the forerunners of the modern greenhouse. These early glasshouses allowed the light to reach the plants, and ventilators ensured that plenty of fresh air was available. Special heating systems used cast-iron piping to carry hot water around the floor areas and thus the orchid house was complete. In this way an environment was at last created in which orchids could grow.

Between the 1850s and the turn of the nineteenth century there followed a utopian era when new orchid species from all over the tropical world poured into Britain and Europe and later the USA, at an unprecedented rate. The botanists could hardly keep up with the work of describing and classifying so many varied and previously unknown species. The method of dispersion was to sell the newly arrived orchids at auction rooms, mostly in London but also in places such as Liverpool, which were near to the docks. Plants would sell for a few shillings a bundle, or for the rarer and much sought after species, bidding would be intense, and prices would soar to unrealistic heights with hundreds of pounds changing hands. Far more money, in fact than was annually paid to the growers employed to look after them. The purchasers of these orchids were, on the one hand, the wealthy land owners or nobility, many of whom had made fortunes in the industrial revolution, and who were at that time laying out their country estates and gardens. Interest in general horticulture was high and orchids especially became a status symbol without a collection of which, an estate was not complete. This era also saw the emergence of several enterprising commercial nurserymen who began to specialise in orchids, sending their own collectors to compete with those of the gentry who still searched for ever more previously unknown orchids.

The largest private orchid collection of that time was built up by William Spencer Cavendish, 6th Duke of

Devonshire, at his Chatsworth estate in Derbyshire. He employed a vast army of growers at the head of which was Joseph Paxton, who was later to be knighted for his design of the Crystal Palace which housed the great exhibition of 1851. Many orchids were introduced into cultivation for the first time through this estate, and their names live on in *Cymbidium devonianum*, *Dendrobium devonianum* and *Oncidium cavendishianum*.

One of the most noted orchidists and botanists of his day was James Bateman. He owned Biddulph Grange, a large estate in Staffordshire. He sponsored George Ure Skinner who became one of the earliest major orchid collectors and who travelled extensively throughout central America. He covered an area from Panama to Guatemala and Mexico, returning regularly to England with large consignments of new plants. This was before the Panama Canal had been constructed and the isthmus was crossed by a mountain railway. On his last trip to Guatemala Skinner crossed on the railway but arrived late at the Pacific coast and missed the steamer to take him to his destination. To pass the time while waiting for the next ship, he decided to do some orchid hunting within the area, but was unfortunately bitten by a mosquito, and died from a fever in three days.

Conrad Loddiges started his nursery in Hackney, London in 1812, dealing in tropical plants and orchids. For nearly 40 years Loddiges continued to pay his own collectors and was responsible for such new introductions as *Cattleya loddigesii* and *Dendrobium loddigesii*. Between 1817 and 1833 Loddiges produced a journal which he called *The Cabinet*, in which he described many of his new-found novelties. This nursery ceased trading in 1852 having introduced many fine new orchids and been instrumental in furthering the knowledge of orchids.

Following on from the publication of *The Cabinet*, *The Gardeners' Chronicle* became the most influential paper of its day and published descriptions of the newly identified orchids. In 1893 *The Orchid Review* commenced publication, and attention was switched from *The Gardeners' Chronicle* to the specialist journal, which continues to be published in six bi-monthly issues each year. Originally started by R.A. Rolfe at the Royal Botanic Gardens, Kew, it is now the orchid journal of the Royal Horticultural Society in London.

In 1808 the firm of Veitch & Sons came into existence dealing in tropical plants, and later in orchids. The main nursery started in Exeter, Devonshire where many orchids were grown. Later this part of the family enterprise was moved to London, with a large nursery in the King's Road, Chelsea. In 1912 Harry Veitch was knighted for his services in horticulture, particularly for his contribution to the great horticultural exhibition that year in London. It was so successful that it became an annual event, known today as the Chelsea Flower Show. Among other orchids, this firm introduced *Odontoglossum harryanum*, *Masdevallia veitchiana* and the early hybrid, *Angraecum* Veitchii.

Sander and Sons of Saint Albans was considered to be among the best if not the largest of the early nurseries. The founder, Frederick Sander, was certainly the most flamboyant personality who counted kings and queens and nobility from all over Europe among his patrons. Started in 1860, this nursery probably sent more collectors to cover a wider global area than any other. At one time it was reported they had as many as twenty-three

29. This early coloured photograph taken in the 1920s shows two 'Maung-We' girls collecting *Vanda coerulea* in north east Burma for the firm of Sander. This famous picture appeared in their books and catalogues in later years.

collectors in the field. Sander courted publicity and encouraged sensationalised stories about himself and his orchids. By the turn of the century Sander had a branch of the family firm in Belgium from where orchids were exported as far as Russia and across the USA, even opening a nursery in New York. The main nursery in Saint Albans grew to vast proportions boasting its own railway siding where consignments of plants would arrive and leave, and truck loads of coal were delivered for the firing of the huge boilers. Visiting dignitaries would alight from a private station adjoining the greenhouses. At its height several hundred men were employed to run the nursery.

The new introductions which flowered in the various establishments were sent to the Royal Botanic Gardens at Kew for formal identification and given a name intended to stand for all time, but which is subject to botanical revision and new classification as knowledge is gained. Hence through the trade links, the nurserymen and the enthusiastic collectors Britain became the centre of the orchid growing world, a position which it held throughout the 19th century.

Thus it was that an entire industry was established and maintained by those early orchid hunters who risked disease and death in previously unexplored lands to satisfy the lust for exotic orchids by those who could afford them. The heyday of the early collections lasted until the First World War. Then the lack of man-power and unavailability of fuel to heat the greenhouses caused the decline of many of them. As the great estates, which once must have seemed so permanent and indestructible, became broken up, many without a surviving heir to carry on, so the orchid collections were lost. During the first war the nurseries turned their greenhouses over to food production, and orchids had to take their chances in unheated areas.

30. Throughout the Victorian times and up to the 1920s one of the most popular methods of buying and selling orchids was by auction. On Friday afternoons for many decades, Protheroe and Morris held auctions at their salerooms in Cheapside, Covent Garden, London. They produced a weekly catalogue of what they had to offer. These old catalogues are highly collectable today as they give an insight into what was available.

The first tropical orchids to be imported were a source of surprise and wonder. Their reproductive system was not understood and botanists were convinced that orchids would never hybridise. The first individual to be accredited with hybridising of orchids was John Harris, an Exeter surgeon. He was a regular visitor to the nursery of Veitch and Sons in that Devonshire city, and suggested to their head grower John Dominy, how he thought orchids could be pollinated. This resulted in the first man-made hybrid being flowered in 1856. It was named *Calanthe* Dominyi, and although not a particularly well-known or showy plant, it proved that orchids could be raised from seed. The work started by Dominy was continued by his successor, Seden, then taken up by most growers of the day. In this field the amateur growers were equal to the professionals, and as a flurry of excited expectation rippled through the orchid fraternity, hundreds of crosses were made, often with orchids quite incompatible with each other. In this way knowledge was gained as to which orchids would cross breed, and it was found that intergeneric hybrids could be made with related groups of orchids, to produce new hybrid genera, as is not possible in any other plant family.

With no knowledge of mycorrhiza, at first the early hybridisers were baffled when the mountains of fertile seed so readily produced refused to germinate and grow. Early attempts which yielded some success, placed the seed on the surface of a 'Mother Plant', where a few seedlings would germinate. But where thousands of tiny seeds were sown, this small return could not be understood.

The problem remained little changed until the end of the nineteenth century (1899), when it was realised that orchids lived in association with a microscopic fungus, which could be found co-existing within the root system and was often present in the compost

31. Joseph Charlesworth was the first nurseryman to raise orchid seedlings in large quantities. As early as 1913 he was using the newly discovered laboratory techniques and by 1920 full production of seedlings growing artificially in flasks had been achieved.

of an established plant. The fungus was capable of releasing the basic nutrients that the seed needed to germinate, establishing a symbiotic relationship between the growing seed and the fungus. This explained the early partial success with seed which had been sown around the base of a 'Mother Plant'. Those individual seeds which became infected with the microfungus, or mycorrhiza were the ones which could germinate and grow.

Finally, the problem which had confounded the growers for nearly fifty years, was solved by Noel Bernard, a French scientist who published a series of papers showing how the fungus could be isolated and used to germinate orchid seed. This was the first breakthrough, and his findings showed that seed which had been inoculated with the fungus germinated and grew more vigorously than those which had no fungus. This important discovery paved the way for further research in this field. Leading nurserymen were quick to take advantage of this new found knowledge, and so the first mass production of orchids on a large scale began.

A leader in this field was the firm of Charlesworth & Company at Haywards Heath. Here they maintained greenhouses full of seedlings all raised by the symbiotic method. In the 1920s the process was further advanced by Dr Knudson, a scientist in the USA. He successfully analysed the nutrients which the fungus was producing and provided these artificially by suspending them in an agar jelly and sowing the seed on this medium. The problem now was to ensure that the right fungus was isolated, and to maintain it in a pure strain, without it becoming accidentally infected with other foreign fungi. As we know, the atmosphere is full of microscopic spores and any one can contaminate a culture and ruin it completely. By using Dr Knudson's method the fungus was bypassed with far greater success. His formula was for sale at £500, which was a vast sum in those days. Nevertheless, there were several buyers, and those nurseries who were first to acquire the formula gained a huge advantage over their competitors. This became known as the asymbiotic, or artificial method, of raising orchids, and is still used, with modifications today.

Over the years refinements of this method have resulted in better plants being raised in less time. Where it once took six or seven years to bring a plant to flowering size, this is now achieved in three to four years. This speeding up of production has greatly reduced the price paid for flowering plants. The raising of seedlings provides new hybrids with greater variety, because no two seedlings from the same parents are ever exactly alike. Each is an individual clone.

In the 1960s a further advancement was made by Prof. G. Morel in France. By culturing a few single cells of growing tissue from a *Cymbidium* growth he was able to multiply them. The pieces of living material, called meristems, were then grown on *in vitro*, and when flowered proved to be identical replicas of the 'Mother Plant'. The first nursery to accept this new challenge was Vacherot & Lecoufle in France. They made great strides using many of their finest quality orchids to produce meristemmed copies. Plants which had been rare and only occasionally for sale through the slow process of back bulb propagation, could now be made available in vast quantities, opening up a universal market for the first time.

This mass propagating method also had a great impact on the cut-flower trade. It improved quality control and enabled cut-flower cymbidiums to be produced to order, flowering for special occasions with the required colour and number of flowers on a spray.

It was the Victorian hybridisers who were the first to note that after a few generations of breeding, they would often be confronted with sterility. For reasons which they were not aware of, they had produced sterile plants which would not give viable seed. They termed these hybrids 'mules', and called hybridizing 'muleing'. Today we understand this has to do with the chromosome count, which can change through cross breeding. Chromosomes carry the genes which contain the DNA which decide a plant's characteristics. In nature, most plants are termed diploids, with an even number of chromosomes, and go on to breed further diploidy in the hybrids.

Most naturally occurring species and their hybrids are diploids, (2n) having an even number of chromosomes. Hybridising can create plants with an uneven number of chromosomes, and these can be triploid (3n) which do not usually go on to breed further. Tetraploids (4n) with twice as many chromosomes are also produced occasionally and these show a much greater vigour with improved substance. By treating infertile orchids in the laboratory, the genetic makeup of the young plants can be altered to make them fertile. Orchids can also have their chromosome count changed with colchicine treatment. Colchicine is an extract derived from the Autumn Crocus, and when the meristem is exposed to it, it has the ability to change the chromosome numbers. Diploids are turned into tetraploids to improve their substance, and make them available for further breeding. In this way previous cul-de-sacs in breeding have been opened up to present new and exciting possibilities. Phragmipediums in particular, have benefited from this scientific approach, to such an extent that there has been a complete revival of the genus, with amazing new hybrids being raised at an unprecedented rate. This has been a welcome breakthrough with a genus which, to date, has resisted all attempts to benefit from meristemming. This is also true of their close relatives the paphiopedilums, which reasserts that these orchids are distinct and different. Phalaenopsis, on the other hand, are difficult to reproduce conventionally but have responded to meristemming very successfully.

These modern techniques ensure that the future shines brightly for orchids, but there is still a long way to go with genetic engineering and who knows what previously unsuspected achievements the flower scientists will create for us in the future.

33. *Cymbidium* Valley Bride 'Honeymoon' was first registered in Australia in 1995. Its ancestry can be traced back to the first hybrid C. Eburneo-lowianum. The result of one hundred years of selective breeding.

Chapter Three

Hybridising and Conservation

When Charles Darwin published his theories of evolution, the old long-held beliefs that every living thing had remained the same since the Creation, were shattered. We now understand that living organisms are continually evolving with minute changes occurring over millions of years as the environment and surroundings change. Some species evolve quicker than others, while those which are too slow or unable to change become extinct. We can see many instances where orchid species are distinct from each other, and yet must have evolved from an original ancestor, later to diversify down separate paths. Global upheavals may have created climate changes which allowed plants to diversify and adapt. As continents have broken up and shifted, vast distances would eventually separate species, only to be brought closer together once again, by further changes to the land masses. Where such movement of species occurs naturally, orchids

32 (Opposite). *Cymbidium* Eburneo-lowianum. The first *Cymbidium* hybrid raised by Veitchs' at the Chelsea nursery. A cross between C. *eburneum* and C. *lowianum*, this hybrid first flowered in 1889 and caused a sensation amongst orchid lovers.

which bloom at the same time will often share the same pollinator, and natural hybridisation takes place. This in itself is a form of speeded-up evolution, and while it does occur among orchid species in the wild, it is unusual and always results in infertile hybrids 'mules'. In evolutionary terms these instances are mistakes, and the hybrid is destined to die out while the species survives to continue the pure line.

In the 1850s British nurserymen were experimenting with the hybridisation of orchids and by careful selection of related species produced fertile seed. For some years John Dominy, headgrower at the nursery of Veitch & Sons, was alone in this field, until others followed upon his success. However, it was at first believed that orchids would only breed through one generation and that all resulting hybrids would be sterile, thus the term 'mule' was used to describe the first crosses. Later it became apparent that second and even third generation hybrids were possible. Today with knowledge of chromosomes and genetics we can take hybridising much further, to produce highly complex, intergeneric hybrids combining as many as seven genera. Among the *Cattleya* alliance there is the genus *Potinara*, made up from *Brassavola*, *Cattleya*, *Laelia* and *Sophronitis*. A well known genus among the *Odontoglossum* alliance is *Vuylstekeara*, made up from *Cochlioda*, *Miltonia*, and *Odontoglossum*. The result of all this excessive and almost compulsive breeding is a continuous outpouring of unparalleled beauty in a bewildering variety which appears to know no bounds, and which has continued unabated for nearly 200 years, yielding further surprises at every turn. Orchids have proved to be the most easily inter-bred plants on earth.

By the turn of the nineteenth century it had become apparent that the hybridising of orchids was going to lead to greater things, and that a register would be required to keep track of the numerous hybrids now being raised, and to avoid confusion with the naming of these new plants. In 1901 Frederick Sander started the Orchid Hybrid List, a register of every new hybrid, which has continued to this day. Now under the auspices of the Royal Horticultural Society in London, it has become the authority for the registration of orchid hybrids world-wide, and lists over 100,000 hybrids. Today this is available in volume form, or on CD Rom. The register is being added to at a rate of over 1,000 entries per year.

Any number of seedlings which are raised from a single cross, will all bear the same registration name. Thus all seedlings from *Odontoglossum bictoniense* x *Odm. cervantesii* will be called *Odontoglossum* Freckles, even though each one will be individually different from the next. The more complex the hybrid, the greater can be the differences between individual plants, or clones. An individual clone can be given a varietal name of anyone's choice, which would read, *Odontoglossum* Freckles 'Your Choice'. Clones produced by mass-propagation retain the same varietal name, as with *Vuylstekeara* Cambria 'Plush', except in very rare instances where the occasional mutation appears which is obviously different from the original clone, as happened with the yellow form of Cambria 'Plush'. When this happens the varietal name is changed, in this instance to *Vuylstekeara* Cambria 'Yellow'. The generic name, *Vuylstekeara* and the grex (a hybrid name) Cambria, remain the same. Only the last, varietal name changes to avoid confusion with the variety 'Plush'.

For the top hybridisers of orchids, one of the greatest rewards is to have their hybrids recognised by an awarding authority. Throughout the world there are many societies and

34. *Vuylstekeara* Cambria 'Plush' FCC/RHS and Cambria 'Yellow'. Mass production by tissue-culture has resulted in colour sports occurring, such as the orange form on the right.

bodies which grant awards to the finest orchids, based on quality and originality of blooms.

Awarded orchids carry the initials of the award after their name, as in *Vuylstekeara* Cambria 'Plush' FCC/RHS. The first initials stand for First Class Certificate, and the second tell us that it was awarded by the Royal Horticultural Society. If the same plant was also awarded in the USA, it would read; FCC/RHS/AOS, the latter for the

American Orchid Society. Other most commonly seen awards include the Award of Merit, AM/RHS, and the Highly Commended Certificate from the American Orchid Society, HCC/AOS.

These top awarded orchids are often mass-produced, or meristemmed, to make them available on a world-wide market. This has also resulted in the world's finest orchids becoming available at reasonable prices, well within the reach of the hobby grower. This is in sharp contrast to years ago, when vast sums would be paid for an individual superior clone, or even a backbulb, which would take years to flower. When the first orchids were meristemmed for a mass market, it was thought that this would lessen the production of new hybrids from seed. But this does not seem to have happened, and today there is the choice of buying a mass propagated plant of top quality, or an individual seedling for around the same price. Where Britain once led the world in hybridising, followed by the

35. At the beginning of the 20th century one of the most famous orchid nurseries was that of Charles Vuylsteke at Lochristi, Ghent, Belgium. Here he specialised in raising odontoglossums and one of the creations was the tri-generic hybrid, *Vuylstekeara*, named in his honour. Alas, the nursery has long gone but the plants that he created live on as his memorial.

USA, today the centres have shifted to Australia, New Zealand and Japan as well as Thailand and Singapore. With an ever growing world-wide market, these countries are extending an already huge and varied choice. There are now more orchid nurseries throughout the world catering for an ever increasing interest in growing orchids. Holland has become the world's largest producer of pot-plant orchids. In response numerous societies have evolved where hobbyists can meet and display their latest floral achievements.

The wild populations of tropical orchids were once thought to be inexhaustible. The nineteenth century orchid hunters stripped areas bare, even chopping down trees to remove every last plant. In many instances complete colonies were wiped out within days of their discovery. It was not always known whether further wild populations existed or not, but it was considered much better for the orchids to be transported from their native habitats and placed in the Victorian greenhouses, where their beauty could be admired, and their every need catered to by dedicated growers. It was pompously, but genuinely believed by some, that the tropical orchids had remained undiscovered for so long because the Creator intended them for the sole pleasure and enjoyment of the Victorians. Only the enlightened European mind had the ability to appreciate their flamboyant beauty and unique qualities and so they were fulfilling the orchids' destiny by bringing them to Europe. This was a form of preservation but without thought for the long term survival of the orchids.

The Victorian ideal was short lived, however. The intervention of the First World War caused the decline of the large collections, and the tenuous ideal of the orchid species in Europe became their demise.

Who can say whether the orchids which were stripped out from the world's tropical forests in the nineteenth century, would still be here in the twenty-first? During the twentieth century 90% of these areas have been cleared of their trees for the timber industry, either way the orchids, along with all other forms of life which depend upon the forests for their existence, would have perished. Habitats are further threatened by agriculture, mining activities and other ways in which humans interfere with wildlife. Where orchids still exist close to crops, the systematic use of insecticides kills pollinating insects as well as harmful pests, which can also have a direct effect on their survival.

Globally, the ultimate survival of the tropical orchids may depend upon the formation of national parks and nature reserves where conservation can be practised, allowing the orchids to grow in their natural homeland along with all indigenous flora and fauna. This is true conservation where the long term future of the orchids can be given paramount consideration.

Orchids are great opportunists and where permitted, will quickly recolonise an area where they have been previously destroyed. In Britain, as elsewhere, native orchids are among the first to recolonise disturbed land, and in early summer brighten roadside verges and waste land where the poor soil inhibits other plants. These areas have therefore become important areas of conservation for plants such as *Orchis mascula* (Early Purple Orchid) and *Orchis morio* (Green-winged Orchid) which find sanctuary there since the loss of the diversity-rich flower meadows which they once covered in their tens of thousands.

36. *Dactylorhiza praetermissa* the Marsh Orchid grows alongside the other wild flowers in soil which is undisturbed and allowed to return to nature.

Countries world-wide approach conservation in different ways. Where national parks have been created and wardens enforce the rules, orchids may be safe from illegal collection. But even here, human nature being what it is, the promise of high prices for rare species remains a great threat. China has only recently welcomed foreign botanists into its territory, and in the 1980s this resulted in a range of exciting discoveries of paphiopedilums the like of which was not even suspected. These extraordinarily beautiful species caused the sensation of the century, but within a few short years of their being legally introduced into cultivation, were systemically collected out, and whole colonies removed from their habitat.

In a supreme effort to eradicate such poaching and amongst growing concern, in 1973 a Convention of interested parties was held in Washington, USA, which formulated the protection of endangered flora and fauna world-wide. Under the title of the Convention on International Trade in Endangered Species of Wild Fauna and Flora (CITES) those orchids considered to be in the greatest danger of extinction were placed on an Appendix 1. which

37. *Paphiopedium tigrinum*. A newly discovered species from China, this was introduced into the western orchid world as recently as 1990. The full extent of its natural distribution is not known but overcollecting will certainly reduce this plant in the wild. It is important that newly discovered species should be raised from seed in cultivation with the long term prospect of re-introducing them to their native habitat.

banned their export. Other orchids, considered not so endangered continue to be exported under licence, and this is strictly controlled. Whilst this legislation has to be applauded, it has not always had the desired effect. Where orchids abound in forest areas being cleared of their trees, because of their rare status, no licences are permitted for their removal, so they are left to rot *in situ*. In orchid growing countries the restrictions have had a detrimental effect on the breeding programmes for these orchids, where it has interfered with the legitimate trade in nursery grown stock. Developing countries, on the other hand, are able to nursery raise seedlings with a view to selling home bred stock, as distinct from wild-collected plants. This has advantages over raising the same species outside of their native environment, it is cheaper and quicker, but it also presents problems for the authorities where nursery-raised plants cannot be distinguished from wild-collected.

Chapter Four

How to Grow Orchids

If you are just getting started with orchid growing, it may be easier to commence with a few choice plants in the home. Later, as your collection and enthusiasm grows you may prefer to extend into a greenhouse or conservatory where conditions nearer to the orchids' natural habitats can be achieved. This is the main difference between growing orchids in the home, where the plants live with you in an environment which you find comfortable. In the greenhouse the conditions are created to suit the orchids. The latter is more demanding and involves extra cost, but is also extremely satisfying and allows a greater variety of orchids to be grown together.

There is hardly any place within the home where a few orchids cannot be grown successfully. Ideally, a south-facing window can be used to create a small growing area for those orchids such as odontoglossums which like good light all year round, provided there is some shade in summer. Low-light orchids, such as phalaenopsis, will do well in a northerly aspect with the minimum of shade during the summer. East and west facing aspects will also provide a winter home for those orchids, such as cymbidiums, which can spend the summer growing season out of doors. Generally, orchids are shade loving plants which need to be kept out of the sun during the summer, but can be given full light in winter when the sun's rays are not strong enough to do any harm by burning the leaves.

Having decided upon the best window aspect you can set up a small growing area consisting of a humidity tray which is a shallow water-holding tray filled with about 2cm of expanded clay pellets. These items are easily obtainable from garden centres and are available in a range of colours and designs. Pour sufficient water into the tray to just cover the pellets. The orchids will stand directly on this so that there is some moisture rising around them, but they are not standing directly in water. The tray can be placed on a table or 'growing cart' kept near the window. A growing cart is a wheeled trolley which enables the orchids to be moved close to the window during the day and moved further into the room on cold winter nights where the plants will be away from any cold passing through the glass.

In addition to the orchids, you can include a few other green plants such as ferns or Impatiens to add variety and colour to the display, but more importantly to provide a good growing environment for the orchids. It would be a mistake to place a lone plant on a window sill and expect it to thrive without any additional incentive. By using humidity trays, you can make your growing area any size you wish, providing there is sufficient light. Provide summer shade by blinds or curtains at the window.

Where you have a choice, use a living room for your orchids, or a room in which you spend some time during the day. Assigning orchids to the spare bedroom which is seldom visited and remains as cold during the day as it is at night, is not the place for orchids unless you are prepared to make it more comfortable. A well-used room such as the kitchen or lounge will ensure that your orchids are looked at frequently, and their immediate needs will be more easily noticed. There will also be a greater difference between the day and night temperature, which is to their benefit. Probably the worst place to put orchids would be the bathroom. This is often the least well-lit room in the house, with very little natural light. Humidity and temperature here are subject to frequent rapid changes which are not ideal. Orchids can be moved around the house until you are satisfied that you have found the right position with enough natural light. Avoid dark corners, and keep plants away from draughts, or radiated heat. The best orchids for indoor growing include the hybrid odontoglossums and miltoniopsis, *Phalaenopsis*, the smaller compact cymbidiums, as well as many of the smaller species which include coelogynes, encyclias and pleiones.

If you already have a greenhouse or conservatory you may decide to grow your orchids there. You do not need a special greenhouse because you can adapt any standard design. Orchids will grow upon benches at a convenient height, and these can be metal trays or wooden slats. The area of glass below the staging can be enclosed with an insulating material or bricks to help retain heat. Ideally, the ground area should be earth with a concrete path. The space beneath the staging can be planted with ground-cover plants to provide a good growing environment from the base up. The ground can be kept wet at all times thus ensuring a constant humidity rising around the orchids. If you are using a solid staging with galvanised trays, you can add expanded clay pellets to this and pour water over it to provide a moist base for your orchids. The greenhouse will need to be shaded during the summer, this will protect the orchids from the direct sun and reduce the temperature during the day. Ventilation will be essential, and on hot summer days it may be necessary to keep the ventilators and doors wide open. The smaller the greenhouse the more rapid the fluctuation in temperature, which can be difficult to control if you are not at home during the day to supervise the greenhouse.

Your greenhouse or conservatory will need to be heated during the winter to maintain a minimum temperature to accommodate those orchids you wish to grow. For the small greenhouse there is a range of electric heaters which are the most satisfactory. Make sure that you purchase a heater which is adequate for the area it has to heat. It is better to have a larger heater working well on a low setting, than to have a small heater turned up high for most of the time. Other heaters which are available burn oil or paraffin, and these are not suitable for orchids. The ethylene fumes which arise from these heaters can cause many problems including bud-drop, and in some cases, can even kill orchids. An electric fan heater can double as a cooling fan circulating the air in summer, which is a great help in keeping a buoyant atmosphere. For heating, place the heater at floor level with a water-filled tray in front of it. Moist air will be drawn forward. Do not allow warm air to impinge upon the plants, which will quickly dehydrate them. In summer, however, the fan can be placed at staging level so that cooling air blows between the plants and moves the leaves.

You will need to establish a daily routine for your greenhouse orchids. In the spring and summer a daily damping down in the morning will create the right humidity and freshen the air. Damping down can be done with a water can in a small greenhouse, but is easier with a hose pipe connected to the mains water supply. Soak the floor beneath the staging, and overhead spray the orchids to give a fine mist over their leaves. This can be increased to two to three times daily during the summer, which will assist in keeping the temperature down. Towards evening, as the temperature drops, the humidity will rise naturally, so damping down should be confined to the morning and up to midday. Keep a check on the temperatures to make sure that your plants do not suffer from overheating during the day. Once the temperature has soared to above 30°C, it can be difficult to get it under control before nightfall. Keep a maximum/minimum thermometer close to the plants and reset it daily. Be sure to give as much ventilation as possible early in the day to prevent a sudden rise in temperature. If you find that it is impossible to control the daytime temperature in the summer, bring your orchids out of the greenhouse and place them in a suitable position in the garden where they will not be exposed to such heat, which can cause them as much stress as severe cold on winter nights. During the winter months, give the orchids all the light that is available. Remove the shading once the sun's power has weaned, and replace it in the spring as soon as the greenhouse begins to heat up. Early spring sunshine coming through the glass directly on to the orchids can very quickly burn their leaves. To prevent this in an emergency, place sheets of newspaper lightly over them to protect them until you can get the summer shading in place. Check your orchids every two to three days for watering, keep a look-out for any pests, which include slugs and snails. Watch out also for new developing flower spikes and support with a cane to prevent them being accidentally damaged. Remove dead leaves from the orchids and other plants to prevent the growth of detritus, and generally keep the greenhouse clean. It is worth spending some time creating the right conditions in the greenhouse, when you will find that the orchids will grow themselves.

While they are active orchids need to be kept evenly moist at the roots and this will mean watering an individual plant perhaps once or twice a week. The nature of the compost ensures that it is swift draining, so that when water is poured over the surface, it runs through the pot quickly and most is lost. For this reason when you water, give a good thorough soaking, flooding the surface of the pot several times to ensure a good wetting. The only way you can do this indoors is to remove the plant to the draining board to avoid flooding the growing area. Those plants which have a sizeable surface area will be easier to water than others which have grown across the pot and may be in need of repotting. Where there is a compacted root ball, watering can become difficult, and it may be easier to plunge the plant into a bucket of water for half an hour or so. Once thoroughly wetted, it should be easier to water from the top again.

Watering orchids is directly related to their state of growth. In the spring most are starting their new pseudobulbs, and this is a time of increased activity when they require plenty of water to maintain their development. Throughout the spring and summer keep your orchids evenly moist. At the approach of autumn many pseudobulbs will be maturing before entering their dormant state. Water can be gradually lessened until the winter, when those orchids which are resting can be allowed to become quite dry. During the winter give only an occasional watering to keep the pseudobulbs plump. This is usually a good indication that the plants are getting sufficient water. A healthy plant should always have plump pseudobulbs, although the oldest ones will shrivel with age when their reserves are used up and this is a natural ageing process. Any amount of water will not plump up these old pseudobulbs because they no longer have any roots of their own to draw up the water.

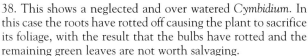

38. This shows a neglected and over watered *Cymbidium*. In this case the roots have rotted off causing the plant to sacrifice its foliage, with the result that the bulbs have rotted and the remaining green leaves are not worth salvaging.

39. *Cymbidium* Pendragon 'Broadmoor'. A fine, healthy plant reflected in the strength of its foliage and production of flowers. The result of correct culture.

If the leading pseudobulbs have shrivelled through underwatering, a good soak will slowly plump them up again. Those orchids which do not produce pseudobulbs such as the paphiopedilums will show signs of dehydrating by the limpness of their foliage, and here the remedy is the same. Shrivelled pseudobulbs can also occur through overwatering, where the roots have become saturated and died as a result, and the pseudobulbs cannot draw up water, so shrivelling occurs. Any plant which is found to have been overwatered needs to be repotted into fresh compost, having first removed all the dead roots which will be found underneath. Progress will not be made until a new growth has developed its own roots and water can be absorbed. This recovery can take up to twelve months if the shrivelled state has been allowed to remain for a long period.

Orchids can be lightly fed using one of the specially prepared orchid feeds available from specialist nurseries and most garden centres. Alternatively, you can use any of the feeds designed for house-plants, reducing the recommended dose to about half strength. By the nature of their natural existence orchids are weak feeders, and can manage to grow indefinitely with the food leaching from an organic bark compost. Those growing in a Rockwool type substance however, have no means of acquiring any nutrients other than what they receive in the feed. A general rule is to add feed, diluted in water as recommended, at every third watering. This can be increased during the spring to every second watering until growth has matured. Those orchids which are resting in the winter

40. A *Cattleya* badly infected by scale which has led to the deterioration of the plant to the extent that it is nearly dead and beyond the point of recovery.

will not require any feed during this time, but those such as the phalaenopsis which continue to grow throughout the year, may continue to be fed at every third watering. When you apply the feed, be sure that the compost is moist. If the plant has become dry give one application of water prior to the feed. Feeding a dry plant, especially in Rockwool, can result in burning the roots. Feeding directly to the pot ensures that the feed is taken up by the root system. You can also feed through the leaves by spraying, or foliar feeding, over the foliage. This is a useful way of feeding orchids which have lost their roots or whose foliage has become yellow through being in need of repotting, or where they have received too much light. This yellowing foliage through lack of nutrients, is different from the natural yellowing through age of the older leaves. An old leaf turning yellow prior to it being discarded by the plant will not turn green again.

In years gone by the feeding of orchids was considered sacrilege, and those who did feed their orchids kept it a closed secret. In some way it was thought to be 'cheating'. Over the years many types of feed have been tried, from cow dung to urine, with others extolling the virtues of soot water. The results of these feeds were usually unpredictable, with no two batches being the same, so it was hard to regulate the strength of feed and be consistent. Orchids often suffered from overfeeding which produced a virus-like flecking in the foliage, or lost their root system through the roots being chemically burnt. For a long time feeding was considered taboo, but today there is a much better understanding of the requirements of orchids, and the specially prepared feeds which are available can greatly improve a plant's performance.

There are basically two types of feed for orchids. One, which is nitrate based is used for

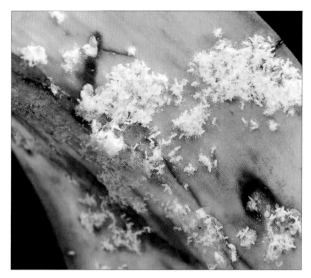

41. There are many different types of scale that attack orchids. Cattleyas are particularly prone to this pest. We see here the woolly white scale and the effect it has had on the foliage.

42. Related to the scales are the mealy bugs. This particular pest will attack most orchids. It is very fond of the soft leafed phalaenopsis. The adult pest can be seen here with its long spur-like tail. Treat both mealy bug and scale with an insecticide or soapy water.

the promotion of growth, and can be applied during the spring and summer growing season. The second is a phosphate feed, which is given in late summer to promote flowering. Feeding is most beneficial when the light is good and there is the opportunity for the plants to convert the feed to their needs. Therefore you can give more applications of feed during sunny weather than you would during long periods of dull wet weather.

Once you get the conditions right for your orchids there is very little which can go wrong. Plants which become sick are usually the result of incorrect culture. The loss of roots is usually the first indication that all is not well with a plant. This in turn will lead to a premature loss of foliage. The result can be a plant with a cluster of leafless pseudobulbs, which although not dead, will be unable to progress unless divided up into single pseudobulbs and potted up in the same way as propagations. New growths will readily be produced on the younger pseudobulbs and progress will be made, but it will take several years for a plant to grow to flowering. You may decide it is not worth the time and trouble when you can replace the sick plant with a healthy one which will provide you with flowers every year. Plants which show black tips to the ends of their leaves can be suffering from cold and damp or the extreme of hot and dry. If your plants are not looking as healthy as they should it points to an imbalance of their conditions and you need to take a long look at the surroundings. Various black or brown marks which appear on the foliage can indicate burning from direct sun, or a fungal infection caused again by cold and damp. Prolonged exposure to an inappropriate environment can result in an attack from virus disease which will show up in the foliage as long black streaks, or with *Cymbidium* Mosaic Virus, diamond-shaped patterns will emerge along the leaf. There is no cure for virus, and any plants with this complaint are best discarded. Virus can be spread from plant to plant by sap-sucking pests such as Red Spider Mite.

Pests which attack orchids include the obnoxious slugs and snails, which are less of a problem indoors than in the greenhouse. They thrive in the moist atmosphere and will travel between the floor to the staging to eat into buds as well as young pseudobulbs and new roots during the night. The best way to catch these is after dark with a torch. Keeping one or two natural predators like toads in the greenhouse will also help to keep the numbers down. Smaller pests are harder to detect and can establish into colonies

43. *Phalaenopsis* flowers will last perfectly for many months but if the temperature is too low, combined with high humidity, then spotting of the flowers will quickly occur. This infection will spread across the flower but improved culture will prevent it from re-occurring.

before being seen. Red Spider Mite is so small it is difficult to see without a magnifying glass. This will reveal small reddish mites on the undersides of the leaves where they cause silvery white patches which later turn black. It is usually the damaged areas which are seen before the pest. Scale insects are also very small, but can be seen, although are not always recognised for what they are. Their appearance varies as there are several different types. The adults can be round, white or creamy coloured with a soft shell, or hard, brown and oval. They all cover themselves in a shell like membrane which can be difficult to dislodge. They damage the leaf surface by sucking the sap and causing yellow patches where they have been. Look for these pests on leaves and beneath the dried sheaths which cover the pseudobulbs of cymbidiums and cattleyas. There is also a woolly scale which resembles mealy bug. The latter covers itself in a woolly-type substance and resembles a small pink woodlouse underneath. Again this is a sap-sucking insect which will leave a trail of yellow patches where it has been. Look for this in the axils of leaves and beneath the sheaths on pseudobulbs. There are numerous insecticides available for treating these pests, including systemic insecticides which render the plant poisonous to the pest. Used with care these pesticides are useful in the greenhouse for eradicating an infestation, but it is unlikely that you would want to use any of them indoors. Here, an alternative and safe remedy is to wipe each affected part with methylated spirits. This is a contact killer and will destroy the pest immediately. It will be necessary to treat the affected plants over a period to ensure that all eggs and future generations are dealt with. On some soft-leafed orchids, the methylated spirits can burn the already damaged leaf, so should be washed off with water after application. Aphids can do much harm on young growths and flower buds. Puncture wounds will grow with the buds, greatly disfiguring the flowers when they open. Aphids are easily removed by swilling off in water. In a greenhouse they can be controlled by an insecticide spray.

44. This shows severe damage to *Cymbidium* flowers by slugs or snails. These pests are very fond of orchids though they seldom eat the plants only the blooms which are quite a delicacy.

45 (Left). This picture shows soft scale on *Encyclia cochleata* which will infect buds and flower spikes and is quickly spread by ants. They derive some nourishment in the form of a sugary substance which the pest gives off.

Many orchids can benefit from summering out of doors where conditions are suitable. This is particularly so where a small greenhouse is overheating and there is no one at home during the day to check on temperatures. Also, orchids being grown indoors may not always receive enough light to promote flowering. Those orchids which will benefit most from being outdoors will be mature cymbidiums, odontoglossums, dendrobiums and other hard-leafed types with pseudobulbs. The soft-leafed lycastes, shade-loving phalaenopsis and paphiopedilums are better left indoors, as also any plants which are flowering. Often a plant which has refused to bloom for years, will burst into flower after a summer in the garden!

Look for a suitable place for your orchids where they will receive the early morning or late afternoon and evening sun, but will be in the shade during the hottest part of the day. Place the plants alongside a hedge, wall or fence, on a bench or on upturned flower pots. Those in pots small enough to be blown over by the wind can be stood together in a seed tray with holes at the bottom so that in heavy rain they are not left standing in water. Try hanging plants in the branches of fruit trees where there is shade, but remember to check them daily for water. In this position the plants can be sprayed regularly and their watering and feeding regime attended to. Remember that the plants will dry out much quicker, and during times of high rainfall may even become too wet. It may become necessary to cover the plants with polythene sheeting during very wet spells of weather, but always remember to uncover them as soon as the sun comes out. Orchids can be placed out of doors in early summer, after all danger of night time frosts have gone. They can remain outside until the nights start to get cold, dropping to below 10°C. If all has gone well, they will be showing plump pseudobulbs larger than the previous ones, and hopefully, with flower spikes appearing. Before placing the orchids back into their winter quarters check them over carefully for any of the pests mentioned and treat accordingly. Now you have only to wait for the flowers!

Chapter Five

Repotting and Propagation

Orchids cultivated in pots will outgrow their containers, and those sympodial types which produce new pseudobulbs, or growths, in front of the previous ones, will fill the available pot surface within two years or so. Inside the pot, their strong roots will use all available space and when the plant is removed, will be found to have a tightly compacted ball of roots. You can see this where a plant which is showing its roots above the rim of the pot, and is pushing itself upwards. Pseudobulbs hanging over the edge of the pot often cannot get their new roots into the compost. It is surprising how many orchid plants are seen in just this state being sold at various outlets around the peak selling times such as the festive season. It is also remarkable how many years an orchid will continue to grow in this crowded and unhealthy state before it starts to decline. Orchids are very resilient and rely upon their own pseudobulbs for reserves when there is no longer nourishment left in the compost. Plants in this state are also extremely difficult to keep wet, as water runs off the top of the pot without penetrating between the compacted roots, so these neglected plants are often showing signs of shrivelling through underwatering. About the only way to get moisture and nourishment to a pot-bound orchid is to soak it in a bucket of water for up to an hour, and spray the foliage regularly, several times daily, to enable some moisture to be taken up through the leaves. You can apply feed in the same way, once a week adding to the water. The best and most obvious solution however, is to repot the plant.

The vast majority of orchids in cultivation are epiphytes, growing upon trees not as parasites, but as air plants. They take nothing from the tree which is used simply as an anchorage to attain a perch upon which to grow. Roots search out amongst the debris and mosses growing upon the tree for nutrients in the form of decaying leaf litter, as well as absorbing moisture from the air. For these reasons orchids are grown in a soil-free compost. There are two basic types of compost, the organic fir bark chippings and the inorganic man-made insulating material Rockwool which is spun glass fibre with the appearance of cotton wool. Both types of compost have their advantages but require slightly different culture.

Fir bark chippings are available from orchid sundry firms as well as specialist nurseries. It is a by-product of the forestry industry, and is the ground up bark of pine tree species. A similar, partially rotted material is used for mulching flower beds, but for orchids the bark is sifted to remove the dust particles, and sold in a dry state. Several grades are available the smallest to suit fine-rooting and seedling orchids and larger chunks for vandas and cattleyas. Bark can be used on its own, or mixed with additional, moisture-holding materials such as *Sphagnum* moss. Rockwool and Stonewool are similar materials which are completely inert and have no food value at all. Feeding orchids therefore

46-55 Basic Repotting Procedures – How to repot an *Odontoglossum* type in bark

46. An *Odontoglossum* in need of repotting. The leading pseudobulb and growth are over the rim of the pot.

47. The plant is removed from its pot to show the extensive root system. The new growth has just started but not yet made its own roots.

48. Remove most of the old compost by teasing it out and gently shaking the root ball.

49. With a sharp knife remove unwanted back-bulbs by cutting through the adjoining rhizome to leave the plants with three healthy pseudobulbs.

50. The plant is now prepared and ready for potting in a moistened bark compost.

51. Trim the old roots right back and reduce the living roots to a length of 15cm. Save the old back-bulbs for propagation.

becomes more essential than when growing in an organic bark mix. Watering is easier as there is less danger of overwatering and the plants can be kept much wetter than in an organic compost. Because there is no decomposing matter there is nothing to cause rot. Two types of Rockwool are available for horticulture use, absorbent and non absorbent. Some growers like to mix the two together to give an even moisture throughout the pot.

It is advisable to determine which type of compost your orchids are growing in, and if you have become familiar with the watering and feeding requirements in that mix, and the plants are doing well for you, stay with it. There is little advantage in swapping from one type of compost to another unless the plants are not progressing or you are having problems keeping it wet. Use one or the other, but do not mix organic material with inorganic compounds, because of the different properties of each one.

Orchid plants will require repotting on average about every two years, when the pot has become filled, or when the compost has deteriorated or become soured and needs to be replaced as a matter of urgency. *Phalaenopsis* and vandas, which are monopodial orchids, will not fill out their pots in the same way as those with pseudobulbs, but they will require repotting into fresh compost when they can often be returned to the same sized pot after root trimming.

The best time for repotting orchids is in the spring when the new growths have started to show, but before the new roots have emerged. In this way new roots can penetrate immediately into the fresh compost. Young adult plants and propagations can be 'dropped on' into a slightly larger pot without any disturbance to their existing root ball. As there is no interference with the plant, this can be done at almost any time of the year, excepting the hottest summer months when the plants can be heat stressed, and the coldest winter months when the orchids are resting. Otherwise, for a complete repot, wait until the spring when new growths are showing. Orchids which are flowering at this time can be left until the flowers have finished at which time the new growth will start. However, if repotting is urgent, it may be best to cut the flower spike and repot earlier. With cymbidiums, the flowers will last just as long if placed in water.

Before repotting starts, decide where you are going to work. If you have a greenhouse or

52. Choose a pot of the right size to allow for two years' growth and crock with polystyrene to improve the drainage.

53. Position the plant and hold firm while filling in with compost. The base of the new growth should be approximately 1cm below the rim of the pot.

potting bench set up, this would be best. If working indoors, you will need a scratch-resistant working surface with sufficient space in which to operate. Have ready a supply of newspaper, a cutting tool and a supply of suitably sized pots. You will also need some crocking material, which may by polystyrene chips, which are ideal, or something similar. If using a bark compost this needs to be dampened beforehand and used in a moist state. It is far more pleasant to use and makes future watering of the plant much easier. If using a Rockwool type compost, be sure to wear protective gloves and a mask against dust particles.

54. Hand firm the bark. Do not use a potting stick as compost which is too compressed will prevent adequate drainage.

55. This orchid will remain in this pot for at least two years. The well-drained bark will last that long without deteriorating. Water the plant after a few days. Repot all sympodial orchids this way, using a fine grade of bark for the fine-rooting orchids, and a coarser bark for the thick-rooting orchids.

56-59 How to drop-on a *Phragmipedium* in Rockwool

56. A completely pot-bound *Phragmipedium* which needs to be moved on in to a larger pot. It can be dropped on without disturbing the root ball. This can be done with bark or Rockwool, but do not mix the two types of compost.

57. This plant has made an extensive root system in Rockwool. There are no dead roots and there is no need to remove any of the old compost.

Young plants which may only just have reached flowering size, and which have no older leafless pseudobulbs and therefore should have no dead roots beneath the surface, may be dropped on without any disturbance to the root ball. To do this tap the plant out of its pot, when it should slide out easily with the compost intact, and select a pot about 5cm larger. Check that the roots are white and alive, and the compost is in a good state. Place a thin layer of crocks in the base of the new pot and place the plant on top to be sure that the base of the plant is level with the rim of the pot. If the plant is too low, add a small amount of compost on top of the crocks. Position the young plant so that the oldest pseudobulbs are against one side of the pot, allowing maximum space at the front where the new growths will eventually grow. In this way there will be sufficient room for the plant to grow on for another year or two. If using a bark type compost, fill this in around the pot and press down firmly with the fingers, pushing against the side of the pot and away from the plant until the compost is about 2cm from the rim. This will ensure that no compost is washed over the edge when giving the first watering.

If you are using a Rockwool type compost, place small handfuls of the medium in and around the plant but do not firm down with the fingers. Instead, give the plant several firm taps on the edge of the work bench to settle the compost and leave it at that. When you have finished the plant should be firm in its pot. The leading growths should be level with the compost and not partially buried by it, or standing proud above. The plant should look comfortable and be stable, which is essential if it is to progress. Orchids dropped on in this way will have been caused little or no stress, and can be expected to respond by developing new roots almost immediately. Remember that a plant can only

58. Position the plant with one hand and fill in with fresh Rockwool but do not firm down. Wear gloves if you have sensitive skin as Rockwool can sometimes act as an irritant.

59. The plant is in its new pot. The Rockwool will swell when the plant is watered immediately after repotting. Re-label if necessary. Any orchid can be dropped-on provided the compost has not decomposed and you do not disturb the roots by dividing or removing any compost.

be dropped on if the compost is in a good state and has not decomposed, and provided that there are no dead roots among the compost. Where either or both of these conditions have occurred, a more complete repotting job needs to be done.

Orchids which have outgrown their containers and whose roots have formed a solid mass, can be extremely difficult to remove from their pots. In some, such as cattleyas, the roots actually adhere to the inside of the pot. If tapping the pot rim of the upside down plant does not release it you may have to cut away the pot. This is easy enough with polypropylene pots which are flexible, but can be more difficult with the rigid plastic, and impossible with clay pots. An alternative method is to slide an old kitchen knife around the inside of the rim of the pot and this will release the plant.

Having removed the plant from its pot, lay it on the newspaper and examine the roots. Live roots will be white, fleshy and brittle, with a growing tip at the end. Dead roots will be brownish, and hollow, the outer covering peeling away to reveal the wiry inner core of the root. Where the roots have formed a solid ball, these need to be teased apart and drawn out to their full length, at the same time removing all old compost from inside the root ball. The dead roots will be found at the back of the plant. They have died quite naturally as the pseudobulb which they supported shed its foliage.

Without roots or leaves the pseudobulb is in a dormant state, supporting the newer growths. If there are more pseudobulbs out of leaf than in leaf, remove the leafless ones by cutting with a sharp knife through the rhizome which joins them. Push the pseudobulbs apart to make it easier to slide the knife between them and cut straight down so as not to slice through the base of the pseudobulb. Retain at least four pseudobulbs and

60. A plant which has grown into two separable divisions can be split at repotting time. Note the two leading pseudobulbs.

61. Using a sterilised knife, cut between the pseudobulbs at the point where you want to divide the plant, and continue to cut through the root ball to separate the two halves.

60-65 Dividing a Cymbidium

a new growth on the main plant, most of which should be leafed. With larger plants which have been growing in more than one direction, divide in the same way to provide any number of plants of a similar size. Take the main plants and trim the live roots to a length of about 15cm. Trim the dead roots back to the base, and discard the waste material in the newspaper, select a pot of suitable size to allow for two years further growth. Pot up each section while holding the plant firmly with one hand and filling in with compost. More will be used than with dropping on, and the plant must be well firmed down. If you are left with a cluster of leafless back bulbs, divide these singly, cut back the roots to 5cm, and place each one in a community pot. Within six weeks new shoots will have started to grow to give, in time, another plant. Before potting up, check that you can see a dormant 'eye' at the base of the pseudobulb. This will appear as a small brown or green triangle at the base and it is this which will start into growth. Some pseudobulbs may be too old to grow, and any which are brown or shrivelled should be discarded. Propagation is only worth doing if you want the extra plants. It can take up to five years for a propagation to reach flowering size, and you may prefer to allot the same space to a plant which will give you yearly blooms.

This basic method of potting is the same for all the sympodial orchids, with or without pseudobulbs. The larger growing orchids such as cymbidiums and cattleyas can be kept to a reasonable size by dividing, but should not be reduced to fewer than four pseudobulbs as this will lessen their ability to flower for some years. Smaller growing orchids such as the compact coelogynes or maxillarias are better left to grow as large as possible without dividing. Larger plants look better and will give a much better flowering display. Pleiones are sympodial orchids but their pseudobulbs are short-lived, and when potting them, which should be done annually, the older pseudobulbs will already have withered and died. The live pseudobulbs will be of the same age, and can be placed in a community pan to give a much better flowering display.

Orchids which have been divided and had their roots trimmed may show some signs of stress, especially if the repotting had been long overdue. Stress will show in the

62. Remove the old compost from the centre of the root ball and trim back all dead roots on both plants.

63. Now your plants are prepared, select the right size of pot for both and place a layer of crocking material at the base. If necessary add a small amount of compost before positioning the plant.

shrivelling of the pseudobulbs, and their foliage may become limp. Keep these plants out of bright light for a while, and spray several times a day to prevent further moisture loss through the leaves. Keep the compost just moist, but not overwet. After two or three weeks new roots will commence from the base of the new growths, and once these roots have been made, the plant can take up moisture and any shrivelled pseudobulbs will fatten out again. From this time, normal watering and conditions can be resumed.

The repotting of monopodial orchids, such as phalaenopsis and vandas follows a similar pattern, except that with phalaenopsis the plants are placed in the centre of

64. Make sure the *Cymbidium* has sufficient space for two years' forward growth, and that the leading growth is on a level with the compost surface.

65. Firm the compost down well with your hands to ensure that the *Cymbidium* is left secure in the pot. Water after a couple of days. New roots will soon replace those which have been lost.

The Progress of Thunias

66. Repot when the new growths appear in the spring. Give the first watering when the growths are about 5-7cm high when the roots will start. Watering too early may cause damping off.

67. By the autumn *Thunia* Gattonensis will produce a beautiful display as their leaves turn from green to golden-yellow before dropping off. At this point stop watering and keep the plants completely dry all through the winter. Repot again in the spring.

68. During spring and summer give plenty of water and add feed every time. By mid-summer these fast growing orchids will have produced their new canes and be in full flower.

69. In the spring calanthes consist of just dry bulbs which have lost their leaves and roots during the winter. The bulbs should be divided and potted up individually either in groups in a single pot or by themselves.

70. Calanthes enjoy a fairly open compost, consisting of bark, perlite and peat. In years gone by they were always potted in farmyard manure. The new growth appears very quickly and the plant starts to enter a rapid growing season.

71. A well-drained compost will enable the roots to penetrate quickly. The plants should be fed every watering, never being allowed to become dry throughout the whole of the growing season.

72. By the autumn, these new growths will have completed and made large, healthy bulbs equal to the previous season, topped by rich green foliage. The flower spikes will soon appear at the base of the bulb. Most calanthes at this time will lose their foliage and should be kept completely dry for the rest of the winter.

73. Top: *Calanthe* Saint Brelade. Below: *Calanthe* Harrisii. During the winter, calanthes produce a wonderful display of flowers entirely from the energy stored in the bulb. These blooms can range in colour from dark red through many shades of pink to pure white.

the pot, which may be no larger than the previous one unless there are sufficient roots to require more space. Phalaenopsis will often resume a semi-pendent habit, their leaves growing at right angles to the pot. Repotting is an opportunity to place the plant in an upright position once again. Phalaenopsis roots can cause a problem because they are often growing outside of the pot, and assume an aerial existence. When repotting, leave these aerial roots outside. If buried in the compost they will suffocate and die. If these aerial roots become broken in the potting process, cut them back at the break. They will heal, and branch out again into the air. These roots will also adhere quite strongly to any surface which they come into contact with, and this can cause a problem when you come to move a plant which has been standing in one place for a long time. This is a greater problem in a moist humid greenhouse, than in the home. It may be necessary to cut the roots where they have become damaged. Occasionally, if there are very few or no roots within the pot, you can trim and bury some aerial roots to hold the plant in its new pot. It is important that the plant is firm. A loosely potted plant which moves about will not progress.

There are numerous epiphytic species which will benefit from growing in hanging baskets, and for stanhopeas it is essential that they are grown in open containers to

Growing orchids on bark

74. This is an exciting, alternative method of growing an epiphyte. The *Bulbophyllum* has been grown from seed in a pot and is now large enough to be treated as an epiphyte, mounted on cork-bark for hanging in the greenhouse. You will need a piece of cork bark, secateurs, pliers, horticulture wire, *Sphagnum* moss and some fibrous material such as coconut fibre.

75. A suitable plant will have a string of pseudobulbs or an upward growing habit making pot culture difficult. Remove the plant from its pot and shake out all the old compost.

76. Make a hole at the top of the bark and push through a wire hook with which to hang the bark up. Prepare a wad of coconut fibre and *Sphagnum* moss mixed large enough to cover the piece of bark.

77. Position the plant over the wad so that it has room to grow upwards. Wire it securely using plastic-coated garden-wire between the pseudobulbs and tighten with the pliers. The plant will quickly root into the moisture-holding wad and on to the bark where it can remain for many years. Be sure to keep the base damp with frequent and regular spraying or dunking. This method of growing is not suitable for indoor orchids.

Creating an Orchid Tree

78 (Opposite above). Choose a tree branch suitable for your display area. This should be from a hardwood like oak or apple, that will take a long time to deteriorate. Fix the branch to a firm base and select about three orchids which are suitable for mounting. You will need a quantity of *Sphagnum* moss, coconut fibre, a length of plastic-coated garden wire, secateurs and pliers.

79 (Opposite left). Carefully position each plant on the trunk anticipating where the flowers will come to make an attractive arrangement. Wire each into place on a base of sphagnum moss and coconut fibre making sure they will have room to grow for many years.

80 (Opposite right). The finished tree will provide an interesting talking-point about epiphytes in any part of the greenhouse. As the plants grow, add further rooting material in front for them to root into. In time aerial roots will be produced.

81 (Above). Spray the tree daily as plants growing in this way can dehydrate quickly. Orchid trees are not suitable as home decoration, and are best in a humid greenhouse or orchid case, where their needs are more easily met.

Potting an orchid in a basket

82 (Above left). Baskets come in various shapes and forms, from wooden slatted square or oblong types to plastic containers. Here, a plastic-coated wire basket is lined with compresssed coconut fibre. Orchids with pendent flower spikes, such as this *Coelogyne massangeana*, are ideal and will benefit from increased space for their roots.

83 (Above right). Remove the plant from its pot and take out the crocks and some of the compost. Avoid disturbing the plant more than necessary as the compost is still good and the thick roots are healthy.

enable their downward flower spikes, which penetrate the compost, to emerge unhindered underneath or through the sides of the basket. Various types of basket can be used. The handyperson can make up attractive wooden slatted baskets of various shapes to suit a plant's individual need, or aquatic water-plant pots can be used. These are made of plastic with open slats and are ideal for certain orchids, particularly those with pendent flower spikes such as gongoras. Among the bulbophyllums are numerous little species which grow with such ease and enthusiasm that within a few short years they can form a complete ball around a hanging basket, completely obscuring the container. Some orchids can be encouraged in this by pegging new growths to the side of the basket in such a way that they grow into a tight ball.

Yet other highly satisfactory ways to grow certain epiphytic species, are on a piece of cork bark, a fibre pole, or a tree branch covered with *Sphagnum* moss or similar moist material in which the plant can root. The plants most ideal for this method of culture include *Oncidium flexuosum*, *Epigeneium amplum*, and any others which produce their pseudobulbs at intervals spread out along an upright rhizome. These plants are extremely difficult to accommodate in a pot, but can look very much at home on bark. After some months, the roots of *Oncidium flexuosum* will form a dense 'beard' trailing down for up to a metre. But this aerial root activity is only achieved by a high level of culture, where

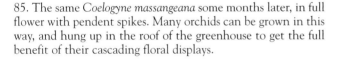

84. Repot as previously described, leaving the plant sitting securely in the centre of the basket with plenty of room to grow. Use plastic string or coated wire secured at three points on the edge to suspend the baskets. This needs to be longer than the height of the foliage.

85. The same *Coelogyne massangeana* some months later, in full flower with pendent spikes. Many orchids can be grown in this way, and hung up in the roof of the greenhouse to get the full benefit of their cascading floral displays.

there is sufficient air moisture for these roots to develop and grow, and this is usually only possible in a greenhouse.

Cork bark is available in slabs from specialist nurseries and orchid sundry firms. You will need a piece several centimetres longer than the height of your plant. Make a hole in one end of the bark and place a wire hook through this for hanging. Remove your selected plant from its pot and trim any dead roots after taking away all the compost. Hopefully, your plant may already have made some aerial roots which can be left intact. If necessary, remove any old pseudobulbs from the back of the plant. You will need to place a pad of moisture-retaining material such as coir, which is used for lining outdoor baskets, or *Sphagnum* moss on to the bark. Position the plant on top of this so that the oldest pseudobulbs are at the lower part of the bark allowing room for the plant to extend upwards. To hold the plant in position use a thin plastic coated wire and place across the rhizome in between the pseudobulbs, tighten and twist. In this way it cannot cut into the soft parts of the plant. Ensure that the plant is held firmly and has sufficient material underneath to hold some moisture. Remember that plants growing in this way will quickly dry out, particularly in the summer when regular spraying will be needed. In addition you can soak the plant in water once a week or so to keep it wet. Within a few weeks you should see notable progress being made, with new roots getting a grip on the bark as well as extending into the air. This idea of growing on bark can be taken one step further and you can put several orchids together on a larger tree branch. The best wood for this is oak or apple, and branches can often be found after a storm laying on the ground. Cut to a suitable size, and mounted on a foot they will make a desirable home for epiphytic orchids, and you can add a few tillandsias or other air plants to give a more realistic effect. Although difficult indoors, this is a lovely way of growing small orchids in a greenhouse or conservatory.

The raising of orchids from seed is a timely and rather erratic procedure which is seldom undertaken by hobby growers. It is usually left in the hands of the commercial nurseries. The sowing of orchid seed is quite complicated and requires some degree of expertise which is acquired by only the most dedicated grower. However, this must not be a stumbling block for anyone wishing to produce their own hybrids, or bring on their own seedlings. There are some orchid nurseries who will, for a fee, sow your own seed and return to you a required number of seedlings *in vitro*, growing in small clear plastic containers on a sterile agar medium, and ready to be potted up in your usual compost. Alternatively, 'hobby flasks', can be purchased at orchid functions which will provide you with just a few seedlings which can provide experience of handling young plants, with all the satisfaction of rearing them to flowering.

At about twelve months from sowing, the young seedlings will be 2cm to 5cm high, each with their own fine roots. Take them carefully from the plastic container either by washing them out with tepid water, or using a small wire hook to ease them out, and place in a saucer of water to which has been added a small amount of fungicide. Carefully wash all the agar from their roots and lay out on kitchen paper to dry. Have ready a few community pots which have been prepared with a fine grade of bark suitable for seedlings, or Rockwool type compost. Some growers like to use finely chopped *Sphagnum* moss, but on its own this does decompose quickly, even though it intially encourages a good root growth. Young seedlings do better in community pots, which can be kept more evenly moist than potted individually in very small pots, which can dry out very quickly and are difficult to maintain in a moist state. Make sure that the prepared pots have been previously watered and are moist, but not too wet. You can handle the seedlings with your fingers or, if you find it easier, use a small pair of tweezers. You will also need a small pointed stick, a pencil or the pointed end of a plant label will do, to make a hole for each seedling. Pick up each seedling carefully at its base, and dip into a rooting compound. Place the seedling in the hole you have made at the edge of the pot. You can place six or eight seedlings around the edge of a 8cm half pot with one or two at the centre. If the seedlings have very long roots which are difficult to accommodate, they can be clipped to a suitable length. These seedling roots are different from those to be made in the new compost, and they will not continue to grow once they are taken out of the agar. Take care not to bury the base of the seedlings too deeply, but tuck the compost around them so that they are firm. Label the plants and place them in a propagating frame, or in a shady corner away from any draughts. Mist the plants daily and keep the compost evenly moist in a temperature recommended for the type you are growing. Allow some fresh air into the propagator, where possible closing down only at night. Progress should be steady, and the critical time will be getting the young plants through their first winter. Check the pots daily, and should any damping off of individual plants occur, remove at once to prevent the spread of any fungal infection. After six months the little plants should have grown considerably, each with its own developing root system. At this stage they can be repotted and, depending upon their size, the largest may go in to their own small pots, with any weaker plants being returned to a community pot.

About one year after having acquired your seedlings, those which produce them should be making up their first seedling pseudobulb. From this will come the next new growth, and when this is growing well, repot once again. At this young stage the plants can be dropped on into a slightly larger pot without disturbing the root ball. From now on repot at six monthly intervals, providing the plants have grown to fill their pots, preferably in spring and autumn. At four or five years old the young plants should bloom for the first time. This will be the climax of several years of growing and waiting, and nothing will compare with the excitement of seeing the first flower spike on a seedling which you have raised. Not until your plants have flowered should they need to be completely repotted, with old compost removed and dead roots trimmed back.

Young plants flowering for the first time will need another two to three years to reach their full potential, and it is surprising how much a flower can improve as the plant becomes bigger and stronger. Also, the flower quality can vary depending upon the time of the year in which it blooms. With some of the complex hybrids within the *Odontoglossum* alliance, blooming can be unseasonal, at intervals of nine months or so. With flowers being produced at different times, it is necessary to see a particular plant bloom over a succession of a few years before you can decide how good it is.

Your seedlings may have all been from one cross, and as they bloom, you will see the variation which comes from a single hybrid. If you made the cross, you may note that one seedling takes more after one parent then another, or that one parent has become dominant. Should you wish to give this new cross a name, this is the time to do it. If the cross was your own, you can apply to the International Authority for the Registration of Orchid Hybrids at the Royal Horticultural Society in London. If your particular cross has not previously been registered, you will be able to select a name for it. If the seedling cross which you have grown was made by someone else, you must obtain their permission if you wish to name it. The nurseryman from whom you purchased the seedlings will be able to advise you.

Bringing on your own plants from a very young age is highly satisfying. However, taking suitable plants on to specimen size is equally enjoyable and is particularly rewarding with the smaller growing epiphytic species, although any plant can be grown on to become a specimen. A specimen plant is one which is left undivided and allowed to increase over a number of years until its full potential is realised. With some species, which readily produce two or more growths from a single pseudobulb, this can be achieved within a few years. There are a number of smaller growing species among the coelogynes, bulbophyllums and maxillarias for example which are good subjects for specimen plants. They tend to retain leaves on the older pseudobulbs for more years, and this is an advantage when you are trying to increase their size for exhibition purposes.

Chapter Six
Orchid Genera

With upwards of 30,000 naturally occurring species, orchids are probably the largest family of flowering plants in the world. In addition, there have been over 100,000 man-made hybrids raised world-wide in the past 130 years. Of the large number of species, only a very small percentage are in cultivation. The orchid family is extremely diverse with plants that range from tiny specimens with often minuscule flowers known as botanicals, and which have little attraction for the home hobby grower. Many more are terrestrials, used to temperate climates, and of little interest due to their unavailability or difficulty of culture. Some of the most gorgeous of the tropical epiphytes are now very rare indeed, and belong either in their native home, where it still exists, or in botanical or specialised collections where they can become part of a captive breeding programme to preserve them for future generations. Therefore the number of easily available, and easily grown, desirable species can be counted in less than one hundred. Hybrids, on the other hand, continue to be raised at an amazing and undiminishing rate. These have become consumer orchids, available through many outlets for a world-wide market to satisfy the house-plant trade. This has brought orchids to the millions enabling everyone to enjoy their fantastic blooms for months on end. However, very few of these orchid plant-buyers will aspire to become growers, or even hobbyists with an interest that will progress beyond the last spray of blooms.

There is little wrong with a market which is developed to give everyone the chance of owning and enjoying beautiful orchid blooms in their home. Those plants which do not last beyond their first flowering in the home are usually sold when pot bound, and in need of attention, which is not always given. These plants are easily dispensed with and replaced with fresh stock, for here there is no danger of depleting endangered plants. Among the many who start with one orchid on their window-sill, a few will graduate to acquiring more and even wishing to increase their knowledge of these beautiful plants. Only then does the complete world of orchids become apparent to the interested persons, and once inspired there is no turning back. In this way the specialist grower is born who will search out those varieties and types which have no place in supermarkets, but which can be found in specialist nurseries and collections of the enthusiast. One of the best places to see these rarer orchids is the specialist orchid shows and exhibitions which are held wherever orchid growers congregate to display their

86 (Opposite). *Cymbidium* Cotil Point. This is one of the large, modern pink hybrids. It is a mid-season variety producing huge, long-lasting flowers of rich texture and colour.

gems. Other sources of interest are botanical gardens which often house many of the rare species which cannot be seen elsewhere. It is at this stage that the whole amazing spectrum that is orchid flowers begins to open up, prompting once again the question, 'How can these all be orchids?'

Apart from the natural species which are so lovingly grown by those fortunate enough to have obtained them, are numerous hybrids from years gone by, which still retain a place in the modern collection. These older hybrids often become overlooked and sacrificed for the newer, bigger or better types, regardless of their timeless qualities, which should ensure them a place in collections for ever. Some older hybrids have become classics and have outlived many of the later varieties. They have stood the test of time and like *Vuylstekeara* Cambria can be found today produced in their hundreds of thousands.

For the beginner wishing to start a small orchid collection, the initial selection is still very large and varied. Whatever your personal taste in flowers, it can be fully satisfied with one type or another.

87. *Maxillaria fucata*. A rare representative of this genus which has recently been introduced from Ecuador, where its native habitat is the high cool regions of the Andes.

88. *Cymbidium erythrostylum*. A species from Vietnam and an important parent in hybridising. This plant has had a lot to offer the breeder where there are still opportunities to use it.

Cymbidiums

Cymbidiums rank among the most popular of orchids and are readily available during their flowering season in most garden centres and some supermarkets as well as in the specialist nurseries all year round. Their popularity arises from their large, impressive blooms which come in an abundance of colours and last for many weeks.

Cymbidiums produce rounded, sheathed pseudobulbs which support several long narrow leaves which are evergreen and which become arching along their length, or remain rigidly upright. The plants can be from 45cm to 1 metre tall. The pseudobulbs will remain in a live state for several years after the leaves have been shed. When repotting, they can be removed and propagated from, provided at least four pseudobulbs are left on the main plant. Always maintain a plant with more pseudobulbs in leaf than out of leaf. Too many leafless pseudobulbs can drain the plant, retarding its progress and

89. *Cymbidium* Beaumont. Very large, attractive white blooms with a tint of pink and coloured lips, ensure this *Cymbidium* is excellent for the grower with plenty of room. It is certainly not a window-sill orchid.

90. *Cymbidium* Geraint. A compact growing hybrid which produces lots of flowers in a small space. Excellent for the small greenhouse or conservatory, this plant can be brought indoors when in bloom.

causing the pseudobulbs to become smaller each year. An overcrowded, pot-bound plant can survive for years in a less than healthy state, but when eventually cut to prevent its total demise, the strain of repotting in a weakened state can take it years to recover sufficiently to bloom again. The roots are thick and fleshy and produced in abundance on a healthy plant. Live roots are white with a green growing tip, dead roots are brownish and hollow.

Cymbidiums' flower spikes are produced by the newest pseudobulb, and occasionally from an earlier one, sometimes two flower spikes appear from one pseudobulb. They begin to show in late summer, growing upright to resemble a pencil, whereas new growths which are often produced at the same time, very shortly fan out into new leaves. As they grow the flower spikes will need supporting with a thin bamboo cane inserted near the spike. This will make sure that the flower spike remains upright and cannot be accidentally snapped. As they progress buds will become visible and there can be up to

91 (Opposite). *Cymbidium* Bulbarrow 'Friar Tuck' AM/RHS. A hybrid between *Cymbidium devonianum* and C. Western Rose giving pendent spikes of richly-coloured flowers. This line of hybridising was popular in the 1970s and 1980s in the UK. Recently interest in this line of breeding has been lost although it is still used in Australia and New Zealand.

92. *Cymbidium* Havre des Pas. This is one of the finest of modern hybrids, showing perfection in shape and flower production. These large blooms are usually produced in a European climate in March or April.

a dozen or more. The flowers are among the most long lived, and will remain perfect for up to ten weeks. They come in a multitude of colours, only blue is unknown. Their large, generous flowers 5cm-10cm across, exhibit boldly marked lips with various patterns of spots, stripes and wide bands of rich colouring. The sepals and petals are equal in size, usually self-coloured, but occasionally spotted or brushed with deeper colour. The flowering season is extensive, starting in late summer with varieties continuing to bloom throughout the winter and well into the spring months.

Originally cymbidiums were all spring flowering standards, with flower spikes up to

93. *Cymbidium* Maureen Grapes 'Marilyn'. This represents a new race of summer flowering cymbidiums which have been produced in New Zealand. This breeding produces many flower-spikes on a small compact plant. The spikes do not develop all at the same time but give a succession of flowers over a very long period.

1.2m tall. Miniature varieties became popular and were found to be more free-flowering producing more flower spikes on a plant. These compact blooms on spikes hardly taller than the foliage proved to be more accommodating indoors. Now these two types have become merged until there are varieties of all sizes, giving the hobbyist even more choice. While all are desirable plants, the standards are more suited to an area where there is ample space and headroom for them to grow. Standard cymbidiums do not do well when grown in cramped conditions with insufficient light. In the right situation they have no comparison and in bloom are second to none. The smaller growing

94. *Cymbidium* Rolf Bolin 'Red Velvet'. This autumn flowering hybrid has scarlet, long-lasting flowers.

95. *Cymbidium* Sarah Jean 'Ice Cascade'. Probably the best of the miniature white flowered cymbidiums producing a cascade of small flowers. It easily wins prizes wherever it is entered in flower shows around the world.

compact varieties, are more commonly found in garden centres, being easier to transport and more popular with the home grower. Their smaller stature renders them easier to accommodate indoors when they produce abundant flowers in all the bright and pastel colours for which they are renowned. The newer, summer flowering varieties have a delicate fragrance which is not carried by all the hybrids.

These are cool growing orchids which require a temperature range of between 10°C and 25°C. The minimum winter night temperature should not drop much below 10°C, and during summer nights this will be nearer 13°C with the natural warmth in the greenhouse or home. Winter daytime temperatures should rise by at least 10 degrees, to a maximum summer daytime temperature of 30°C. Temperatures outside of this range will cause stress through cold or heat, and this can manifest itself in premature leaf loss, or bud drop, where the buds turn yellow and drop off just when they get to the point of opening. Plants exposed to higher temperatures can suffer from heat stress and will do better when placed out of doors in the summer to be given a cooler environment. This will also benefit cymbidiums which are being grown in the home for the remainder of the year, and may not be getting as much light as they need in order to flower well. Ideally, cymbidiums like light shade in summer and full light in winter. Water all the year round to keep the pseudobulbs plump, but give less in winter when they will take longer to dry out. During the summer cymbidiums enjoy overhead spraying, if out of doors this can be done with a hose pipe, spraying water underneath and through the leaves as well as over them. This will deter Red Spider Mite which can breed on the

96. *Cymbidium* Showgirl 'Anne'. Another compact growing *Cymbidium* which will produce its flowers in winter and spring. A very long-lasting orchid if the atmosphere is kept cool and dry.

undersides of the leaves and to which cymbidiums are prone. During the spring, summer and autumn months add feed to every second or third application of water. Repot as necessary about every other year, in the spring, or when they have finished flowering. Plants can be tidied up at repotting time by removing any broken leaves or black tips which appear on the older leaves, and by stripping the old bracts covering the leafless pseudobulbs which can harbour pests such as woodlice or earwigs. Indoors, keep the foliage clean and free from dust by wiping occasionally with a damp paper towel.

Cymbidium species originate from India, Burma and Thailand as well as parts of Australia, China and Japan. The greatest concentration of species occurs in the Himalayas where the plants grow mainly as epiphytes, but can also be terrestrial, growing in the leaf litter on the forest floor. Most species are rare and belong in specialist collections. The hybrids far outweigh the species for the hobby grower and it is these which have produced the multitude of colours and sizes.

97. *Odontoglossum pestcatorei*. One of the most beautiful and varied of the *Odontoglossum* species which has contributed much to hybridising and, although seldom seen in collections today, was widely grown by our Victorian ancestors.

Odontoglossums and related genera

Odontoglossums are at the head of a vast complex group of beautiful intergeneric hybrids which have arisen from the naturally occurring related species. They have been interbred for almost 100 years to create the bewildering variety now in cultivation. These are amongst the most popular of orchids, prized for their highly decorative flowers, often produced on tall flower spikes from modestly sized plants. While in their plant structure all *Odontoglossum* types are similar. In their flowers they show great

98. *Odontoglossum* Geyser Gold. This is a hybrid from *Odontoglossum (Lemboglossum) bictoniense* var. *album*, which has produced pure yellow flowers devoid of any other colour pigmentation.

99. *Odontoglossum hallii*. This species from Colombia, with its pale yellow sepals and petals with brown markings, is a high altitude, cool-growing plant. It has a strong perfume similar to *Buddleia* which seldom carries through when hybridised.

individuality to such an extent that there is hardly a typical *Odontoglossum* type flower. The true *Odontoglossum* hybrid carries flat, rounded flowers with sepals and petals of equal size, crisped and wavy-edged with a neat lip. The colouring starts with pristine white and ascends through yellow, pink to deep red and mauve, bordering on the elusive blue. The flower can be self-coloured, lightly spotted or densely patterned with intricate markings richly displayed, singling them out as the most decorative of the cultivated orchids. Breeding with closely related genera has given rise to a kaleidoscope of fanciful colours as well as changing flower shape with dramatic results.

Among the most favoured intergeneric hybrids are odontiodas (*Odontoglossum* x *Cochlioda*) which are indistinguishable from odontoglossums, but were originally more richly coloured. Six to eight 6cm wide flowers are carried on flower spikes 30cm to 1m tall. Their flowering is erratic throughout the year; the plants producing a new pseudobulb every nine to ten months and flowering soon after. Odontocidiums (*Odontoglossum* x *Oncidium*) mostly produce longer flower spikes up to 1m or more and their richly decorated flowers are often smaller. Some very beautiful hybrids have been raised from the species *Oncidium tigrinum* and a number of these with 6cm wide flowers exhibit rich yellow and brown colouring with large, flared yellow lips. Among odontonias (*Odontoglossum* x *Miltonia*) the typical flower has a much larger lip influenced by the *Miltonia* parent, and this is usually very prettily marked. As the hybrids become more complex, combining the generic names becomes difficult, and so

101 (Above). *Odontocidium* Russiker Gold. The fascination of a pure yellow flower covered in continuous intriguing patterns, spots and curves, makes each flower individual rather like a fingerprint.

100 (Left). *Odontocidium* Hansueli Isler. An attractive hybrid bred from *Oncidium tigrinum* which has proved to be the dominant parent, as can be seen in the patterning and configuration of the flower.

they are given latinised people names, such as *Vuylstekeara (Cochlioda* x *Miltonia* x *Odontoglossum)* named for Mr Vuylsteke, a Belgian grower who produced the first cross of the genus. One *Vuylstekeara* in particular (*Vuylstekeara* Cambria 'Plush' FCC/RHS) has become one of the most successful orchids of all time and has been meristemmed by the million to such an extent that mutations have appeared which are distinct from the original plant, example (*Vuylstekeara* Cambria 'Yellow'). Beallaras (*Brassia* x *Cochlioda* x *Miltonia* x *Odontoglossum)* add a further dimension to the equation by the inclusion of

102. *Wilsonara* Japan. This hybrid has been raised from one of the long-spray oncidiums, *Onc. leucochilum*, to give many flowers on a branching spike which can be anything up to a metre long.

Brassia, the Spider Orchid grown for its long narrow petals and sepals. The influence of this genus can often be seen in the pale, pre-dawn colouring of the hybrids whose petals and sepals have been extended and narrowed to produce a perfect, star-shaped flower of great charm.

Among the wilsonaras (*Cochlioda* x *Odontoglossum* x *Oncidium*) are some lovely hybrids which produce tall, branching flower spikes with a flurry of dainty, starry-shaped flowers in a riot of colour. Many more bewitching crosses are readily available to the hobbyist through the specialist nurseries and a few selected clones from other outlets throughout the year. All can be grown together, although those with a strong influence from the miltonia will succeed in warmer climates such as Florida which does not suit the remainder of the family.

Odontoglossums and their allies are evergreen plants which produce green oval pseudobulbs with a pair of long, narrow leaves at the apex and one shorter pair at the base. The flower spikes emerge from either side of the leading pseudobulb from inside a basal leaf. Their roots are fine and abundant, and for this reason the plants grow best in a fine grade of compost. Grow in as small a pot as possible, overpotting can quickly lead to overwatering with the loss of roots and possibly the plant. Propagation is not as easy as with other sympodial orchids, the older pseudobulbs do not readily produce new growths when taken from the main plant. Instead, they should be left on the plant until they turn brown and wither. Only occasionally, if the plant has suffered from premature leaf-loss resulting in a cluster of leafless pseudobulbs, should they be removed before they are dead. Repot odontoglossums in the spring, but not while they are flowering. If necessary, they can be dropped on in the autumn when there is no disturbance to the root ball.

Odontoglossums are cool growing orchids, which with a few exceptions (vuylstekearas/ colmanaras) cannot tolerate very high summer temperatures. They do well in summer from being placed out of doors provided a suitable place is found for them where they will be in the shade for most of the day. Indoors, they should be placed where the temperature will not rise above 24°C, with a night time drop of about 12 degrees. Their leaves will often turn a slight reddish colour which shows that they are getting enough light, and too much shade during the summer will inhibit their flowering. During the winter they can receive all the light that is available, when their temperature range should be from 11°C at night to a maximum 24°C during the day. Water the plants throughout the year keeping them moist, but not too wet and give a light feed at every third watering during all but the coldest of the winter months. Odontoglossums usually keep free from insect pests, but if summering out of doors Red Spider Mite should be watched out for when the plants are returned to their indoor growing area.

These are not difficult orchids to grow and are suitable for indoors or a cool greenhouse. Having originated from high altitude plants they like an abundance of fresh air at all times, but without a cold draught. If growing in a small greenhouse it is an advantage to have some air movement around them. In summer, a cooling fan moving

103 (Opposite). *Odontioda* Panlek. One of the lovely red and orange flowered odontiodas.

104. *Wilsonara* Widecombe Fair 'Burnham'. Produces branching flower spikes a metre and a half long full of star-shaped, brilliant, pink and white blooms.

105. *Beallara* Tahoma Glacier 'Green'. Beallaras are complex hybrids within the *Odontoglossum* alliance. *Brassia* blood makes the plant tolerant of both higher and lower temperatures than is normal for odontoglossums. The long-lasting blooms are among the most attractive within this group.

air through the leaves will prevent overheating. Where a good selection of these superb multigeneric hybrids are grown you can enjoy plants blooming for most of the year, with individual flowers lasting up to six weeks on the plant. Those which bloom during the summer months need to be placed in the shade to prevent the flowers from losing some of their lustre.

Odontoglossum species and their extended family members are epiphytic, high altitude plants originating from the Andean range in Central and South America. Most of them are found today in specialist collections and for the hobby grower the brilliantly coloured hybrids are the most desirable. The species are extremely variable, and this has led to the huge variation among the hybrids developed from separate breeding lines.

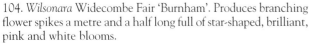

106 (Opposite). *Odontonia* Debutante 'Oxbow'. This is a classic hybrid which has remained popular for many years. It is a primary cross between the species *Miltonia warscewiczii* and *Odontoglossum cariniferum*.

107 (Above). *Miltoniopsis* Jersey. This is a modern, highly-coloured hybrid, one of many which have returned to popularity after being thought difficult to grow. They are now commonly grown as house plants.

108 (Right). *Miltoniopsis* Portelet. This flower has the distinct waterfall mark and heavy dark patterning on the lip which it has inherited from the species M. *phalaenopsis*.

Miltoniopsis

These are the highly decorative Pansy Orchids, so beloved by small, window-sill growers for their compact size, ease of growth and large, flat flowers in gorgeous colours. They are available in great variety all year round from specialist nurseries, and during their summer peak flowering period they can be found in bloom at garden centres. They are undoubtedly one of the best pot-plant orchids requiring little space and the minimum of care.

Miltoniopsis vegetatively resemble the odontoglossums to which they are closely related and will readily interbreed to produce intergenetic hybrids such as *Odontonia*. Previously, all miltoniopsis were classed with the true miltonias, and this name has been retained for the registration of hybrids. Miltoniopsis produce neat plants, with a light, almost bluey-green foliage. The pseudobulbs are rounded and remain leafed for most of their life. The flower spikes emerge from the base of the leading pseudobulb with up to six large, 8cm wide flowers. These range through pristine white, cream and buttery yellow to all shades of pink culminating in rich velvety reds which are among the most vibrant colours found in orchids. Only in the *Cattleya* family can some hybrids compare with the richness of the miltoniopsis. This wonderful range of modern hybrids has come from a relatively few species which are no longer in general cultivation, but are the reserve of specialist collections. The hybrid flowers have petals and sepals of equal size, but it is the large, rounded lip which gives rise to their common name. At the centre of

109. *Miltoniopsis vexillaria*. This is the original species from which all the wonderful hybrids of today have been produced. This species was rigorously collected in Victorian times and loved for its many colour forms.

110. *Miltoniopsis* Plemont Point. A hybrid showing all the good characteristics of a modern flower. The large, heavily marked petals have been inherited from the species M. *roezlii*.

the lip is a bold, butterfly-shaped 'brooch', known as the mask. This design may be confined to the centre or be spread out over the lip. Some of the loveliest examples are those with 'waterfall' patterns, and these are much sought after.

Miltoniopsis are top of the list among the summer blooming orchids, and will often produce a secondary flowering in early autumn. It is not unusual for a plant to produce two flower spikes, one from each side of the leading pseudobulb. These often need supporting with a short cane to prevent the heavy blooms from pulling the flower spike down. Unlike their relatives among the odontoglossums, miltoniopsis blooms will not last if cut from the plant. Within a day or two of being placed in water they will fade and die. On the plant they will last for a good three weeks, and it is best to keep water well away from the blooms, and keep the plant on the dry side to extend the life of the flowers. Nearly all the hybrids are sweetly fragrant, and this is most noticeable in the greenhouse on a sunny morning.

While miltoniopsis do well on a window-sill, they will not grow in isolation, and need the company of other plants around them to provide an all important growing environment. They are shade loving plants, and their soft foliage will quickly deteriorate if exposed to strong light or sun. Naturally pale, be sure to prevent the leaves from becoming yellowish. Too much exposure to strong light will also cause premature

111 (Left). *Miltoniopsis* Rozel. This is a further example from the same line of breeding, where the pattern is a solid mask on the dark lip with a white margin extending into the brilliant petals.

112 (Below). *Miltoniopsis* Rozel. The finer patterning on the lip of this modern hybrid is referred to as 'tear-drop'. It comes from the original two species, M. *vexillaria* and M. *phalaenopsis*.

These two clones of *Miltoniopsis* Rozel show the variation which can occur between hybrids of the same clone.

leaf-loss, which is disfiguring and weakening for the plant. A north-facing window will suit these orchids provided you pay some attention to their temperature requirements. Miltoniopsis do not like to be too cold at any time, and prefer the warmest part of the cool greenhouse, conservatory or room where the winter night temperature does not drop below 11°C or 12°C. On winter days this should have a lift of at least 10 degrees, and anything up to 24°C maximum is fine. Summer temperatures should remain below 25°C for these orchids which cannot stand too much daytime heat. Be sure to find them a cool, shady area where they will grow at their best. Miltoniopsis do not always do well placed out of doors, their softer foliage will suffer from exposure to the elements, and as their flower spikes are developing and blooms opening during the summer months, they are better off indoors. Water miltoniopsis all year round to keep evenly moist, giving less in winter as they take longer to dry out. Their foliage can be occasionally overhead sprayed very lightly during the summer when they are not in flower, but if in doubt leave the foliage dry. Because they are grown in more shade than other orchids, wet leaves will take longer to dry, and this can cause damp spots. Indoors, wipe their leaves regularly with a damp paper towel to remove dust, but otherwise keep the leaves dry, unless the temperature rises above the recommended maximum, when a cooling mist will do nothing but good.

Miltoniopsis are not usually troubled by many insects pests, but you need to keep an ever watchful eye out for Red Spider Mite, which can get on to almost any orchids. Look for the tell-tale silvery white patches on the undersides of the leaves, and wipe clean with methylated spirits before washing off with water. Slugs and snails can do considerable damage to the lush younger pseudobulbs as well as new roots. Plug any slug holes with horticultural sulphur to prevent rotting.

Repot miltoniopsis in the spring, when the new growths are a few centimetres high, which is before the new roots start. Their rooting system is very fine, so a fine grade of bark compost is best, unless you are using the Rockwool type compost. Whenever possible drop on plants without causing any disturbance to the root ball. Miltoniopsis do not like having their roots disturbed, and their pseudobulbs will sometimes shrivel quite badly after repotting, especially where this has been done at any time of the year other than the spring.

In company with the odontoglossums, miltoniopsis do not readily propagate from back bulbs, and their dislike of disturbance should prevent their being removed unnecessarily. Miltoniopsis will grow into considerably large specimen plants, and they should only be divided into smaller divisions when absolutely necessary. One specimen plant will give you a complete flower show on its own and is a never-to-be-forgotten sight!

The species of *Miltoniopsis* from which the modern hybrids have been raised are high altitude plants originating from Central and South America. They grow as epiphytes on the trees in humid, shady habitats. The first flowering of the delectable, pink-flowered *Miltoniopsis vexillaria* in 1873 created a sensation among the orchid fraternity. Discovered a few years earlier in Colombia, it was never very plentiful, and today is a treasured collector's item, while its progeny are numbered in their thousands.

113. *Miltonioides confusa.*
It comes from Mexico
and produces tall,
branching spikes of
attractive, scented
flowers. It will
interbreed with its
South American
odontoglossum relatives.

Cattleyas and allied genera

114. *Cattleya* Bahiana. A small, compact-growing *Cattleya* with interesting flowers which have a splash of colour on the petals and spotted sepals. This is a bi-foliate type produced from *C. aclandiae*.

Riding high at the top of the largest alliance within the orchids are the cattleyas. They preside over a vast radiating web of inter-related hybrids which encompasses many natural and man-made genera. The first include *Sophronitis*, *Brassavola*, *Laelia*, and *Epidendrum*. When combined these natural genera and others, produce such flamboyant intergenerics as *Laeliocattleya*, *Brassolaeliocattleya*, *Sophrolaeliocattleya* and *Epicattleya* in numerous permutations which are just the start. Many more related genera have been added to this vast group, all of which are vegetatively similar, known collectively as cattleyas and treated in the same way. Their extremely large flowers (up to 15cm wide) stand unrivalled, even among orchids, for their magnificent dazzling beauty.

Cattleyas produce distinctive plants which vary only in their size. Miniature varieties containing the diminutive *Sophronitis* can be from 10cm tall, while most of the laeliocattleyas and brassocattleyas grow to 45cm or more. Their pseudobulbs are long and club-shaped, swelling out along their length with either one or two leaves at the apex. These are long and oval, semi-rigid, dark green and are retained for several years. The flowers are born on usually short spikes from between the leaves at the apex of the pseudobulb. Usually, a protective green sheath forms between the leaves and the buds develop inside this. As they grow the sheath splits along its edge to allow the buds to emerge and continue their development. Depending upon the type, there may be from one to six blooms. Typically, the flowers are large, softly textured with narrow sepals and petals much wider with frilled edges. The lip is large and exquisitely coloured or veined, the edges crimped and frilled. The colours start with crystalline white, through the

115. *Cattleya* Portia. This is one of the earliest hybrids produced in 1897 by the firm of Veitch & Sons from *C. bowringiana* x *C. labiata*. A large robust growing orchid seldom seen today, it is well worth a place in any collection of the rare and unusual.

116. *Cattleya* Winter's Lace. A large, white, modern hybrid raised in California where these huge-flowered cattleyas are still very popular.

spectrum to soft pearly pinks and deeper lavender to the incredibly rich purples and mauves. Rich yellows are also numerous, and when combined with deep purple lips these are irresistible. Blue is also apparent, but rare, and much looked out for. Other hybrid combinations, particularly with *Epidendrum*, have created some very beautiful green clones. Smaller varieties, bred with the brilliantly red coloured species *Sophronitis coccinea*, have produced a number of small-flowered, but richly hued hybrids, with fiery reds and fruity oranges complemented by golden yellows and autumnal coppers. Spring and autumn are the two main flowering seasons when these superb orchids vie for attention with a riot of colours and nose-tingling fragrances, each one lasting for up to three weeks.

Cattleyas are termed intermediate orchids, requiring a temperature which is in between the cool and warm growing types. The minimum winter night temperature needs to be no lower than 13°C, rising to 24°C during the day. In summer these temperatures will be correspondingly higher, with a maximum of 30°C by day.

Cattleyas follow a growing and resting cycle whose duration can vary between

117. *Brassolaeliocattleya* Memoria Helen Brown 'Sweet Afton' AM/AOS. One of the most stunning of the green-yellow *Cattleya* type hybrids, which was awarded an Award of Merit by the American Orchid Society.

individual plants. Typically, the new growth starts in the spring with a plant growing throughout the summer and maturing its pseudobulb in late summer or autumn. Often a plant will flower at this time, before commencing its rest for part or most of the whole winter. While cattleyas are actively in growth they need plenty of water with some feed added to every other application. This is gradually lessened through the autumn and discontinued in winter, allowing the plants to become quite dry, but not so dry that their pseudobulbs start to shrivel. The occasional watering will take them safely through the winter. During the remainder of the year they can be lightly sprayed or misted over their leaves.

Cattleyas can be grown in an indoor environment where there is sufficient room for the bulky plants, or ideally in a conservatory or greenhouse where the temperature is controlled and some shade is provided in summer. In winter they can be given as much light as possible, but care must be taken in the early spring when the strengthening sun can easily burn their thickened leaves. They are not well suited to living out of doors during the summer where the cold nights can retard their growth.

118. *Laeliocattleya* Elizabeth Fulton is one of the richest and most brilliantly coloured of the *Laeliocattleya* hybrids.

119. *Laeliocattleya* Ocarina 'Fascination'. Line breeding from the species *Cattleya dowiana* has produced the bright gold petals and huge colourful lip to make a wonderful contrasting flower.

120. *Laeliocattleya* Lake Casitas x Irene Finney. This type, with huge, lavender petals and darker lip, was extremely popular in the 1920s and 1930s in the British collections. Now it is more favoured in the United States.

121. *Laeliocattleya* Pandora Bracey. This hybrid gives a semi-peloric flower where the lip pattern is repeated on the petals in an eye-catching display known as 'splash-petal'.

122. *Sophrolaeliocattleya* Marion Fitch 'La Tuilerie'. A rich, highly-coloured modern hybrid that blooms best in the summer.

123. *Sophrolaeliocattleya* Precious Stones x *Cattleya leopoldii*. A peloric form showing the lip patterning reproduced on the two petals. This modification is highly prized by growers who are interested in unusual shapes and colour forms.

124. *Laeliocattleya* Canhamiana 'Coerulea'. This is a primary hybrid between *Laelia purpurata* var. *werkhauseri* x *Cattleya mossiae* 'Blue Two'. In this cross the *coerulea* forms of both species were used producing the blue colouring.

125. *Laelia gouldiana*. This species from Mexico has deep, richly coloured flowers and, although not as common in cultivation as it used to be, it is well worth looking out for.

126. *Laelia autumnalis.* One of the cool growing laelias from Mexico, this free-flowering species produces several blooms on a long flower spike.

Pseudobulbs of the sympodial orchids are joined by a woody rhizome which is usually below the surface and not noticeable unless you cut through it when dividing a plant. In the cattleyas the rhizome forms a significant part of the plant. It is clearly visible running across the surface of the container with the pseudobulbs arising from it, often forming a long string. Division and back bulb propagation is done by severing the plant in the autumn, cutting through the rhizome while the plant remains in its pot. It is then left undisturbed throughout the winter, and by the spring the back portion will have started a new growth. At this stage the plant can be removed from its pot and the two halves potted separately. The new roots will appear some time after the new growth. The roots of cattleyas are thick and rigid, and when seen outside of the pot are very impressive. It is not uncommon for cattleyas to make roots outside of the pot and these can be regularly sprayed and encouraged to grow. However, when the time comes to repot they can pose a problem, because they will not grow inside the pot. The best time to repot plants which have outgrown their containers is when the new growth is just starting, but while the older roots are still inactive, and can be trimmed back.

Cattleyas can become inadvertent hosts to a number of insect pests including mealy bug and scale. The mealy bug will congregate beneath the dried sheaths which cover the elongated pseudobulbs, as well as in between the pseudobulbs and around the rhizome. Various types of adult scale insects attach themselves to leaves, and both pests leave yellow patches where they have been. They are sap-sucking insects which can weaken a plant if allowed to build up into colonies. Treat these pests with a systemic insecticide or other preparation available from garden centres. If growing indoors, it is safer to use the contact killer, methylated spirits, remembering to wash the affected plants with water after. The blooms of cattleyas are softly textured, and in a greenhouse are prone to damp spots, particularly when the temperatures are low over a few days. To avoid this

127. *Laelia purpurata.* One of the South American laelias coming mostly from Brazil. This orchid has a great many colour variations, all of which are very appealing. The clone has white petals with a coloured lip and usually blooms in the spring or early summer.

128. *Laelia purpurata* var. *sanguinea.* This very fine variety is the darkest and richest of the *L. purpurata,* producing huge, colourful flowers.

keep the plants drier when in bloom, and if necessary increase the heat by a few degrees to dry up the atmosphere and prevent the *Botrytis* spores from spreading.

Cattleya species are extremely variable and can be divided into two basic groups. Those with one leaf and those with two. Each group is distinct, the single leafed varieties being the larger, showier types, and the two leafed, or bifoliate types, having smaller flowers of a more waxy texture, with smaller lips. Among the other related genera including laelias there is the same diversity, all of which has added to the rich assortment of hybrids available today. The species come mainly from Central America and grow as epiphytes, some developing great masses of roots which trail in the air below the plants. *Cattleya labiata* from Brazil, with chocolate-box flowers of pale lavender, was the first to be noticed, creating an unprecedented commotion when it first flowered as early as 1821 and a demand for more of the same.

129. *Laelia purpurata* var. *carnea*. A very attractive variety with an unusually coloured lip. It is as easy to grow as the other varieties of this species.

Dendrobiums

130. *Dendrobium nobile.* One of the most popular of beginners' orchids which will grow under almost any conditions and flower freely. Brightly coloured flowers make it number one for most growers.

This is a huge genus with over 1,200 species spreading across a wide area on both sides of the Equator. They can be found from Malaysia and the Philippines spreading north to India, Burma and China as well as Japan and extending south, through Indonesia, Papua New Guinea, Australia and New Zealand. With such a wide distribution, it is hardly surprising that this is an extremely varied genus. Nevertheless, when confronted with species from as far as India and Australia, with their colossal floral differences, you cannot help but be astonished at the amazing variety. It is almost impossible to describe a typical *Dendrobium*.

From this abundance of species, only a minority are regularly found in cultivation. These are the more showy varieties which hold the greatest attraction for growers. Of

131 (Opposite). *Dendrobium nobile* var. *albiflorum*. Another variety of this lovely species where the pink pigmentation has almost been lost, leaving the dark centre to the lip.

132. *Dendrobium nobile* var. *virginale*. A pure white form of *D. nobile* with no colour pigmentation. This variety grows shorter than the type.

133. *Dendrobium aureum*. A pretty species from India well-known for its perfume. The creamy-yellow flowers are produced along the length of the cane in the spring, after a semi-deciduous rest.

these, even fewer have been hybridised to any extent, and the most successful group of hybrids have all come from the Himalayan species *Dendrobium nobile* and its closest relatives. This has heralded a new generation of delightfully colourful crosses which are easy to grow and flower in a variety of situations. Raised in Japan by Mr Yamamoto, a grower with an eye for shape and colour, these *D. nobile* type cultivars are affectionately known as Yamamoto dendrobiums. The plants are readily available in a wide variety of colours with 6cm wide flowers in specialist nurseries and in some garden centres during their spring flowering season. These popular hybrids have, to a large extent, taken over from the original species, mostly from the Indian continent, which so frequently graced collections a few years ago. Now these species are in decline in cultivation, due to importation restrictions which go hand in hand with their increasing rarity in the wild.

Other dendrobiums, particularly miniature species from Papua New Guinea such as *D. cuthbertsonii* are coming to the fore, being prized for their compact size and incredibly colourful flowers, and their willingness to produce good hybrid forms. A group of large-flowered species native to Australia including *D. bigibbum* and its varieties, are also becoming more popular and providing showy, white to mauve hybrids of compact size. These newer hybrids are doing much to popularise and change the face of a genus once dominated by the Indian species.

Dendrobiums are easily recognisable by their elongated pseudobulbs which are commonly known as canes. These canes can be a metre or more long and thin, (*Dendrobium aphyllum*) where they assume a drooping habit, or of moderate length 30cm

134. *Dendrobium* Thwaitesii 'Veitch'. A very old hybrid with beautiful yellow flowers, still easily grown and in demand today.

135. *Dendrobium* Oriental Paradise. Another hybrid with beautiful, tipped petals on large, well-rounded flowers which are produced along the whole length of the cane.

(*D. nobile*) and upright stance, or at 5cm much shortened and dwarf-like (*D. cuthbertsonii*). They can be smooth or knobbly along their length with intersections where the narrowly-oval leaves appear. Some are leafed along their entire length (*D. nobile*), while others produce leaves from the top half of the canes (*D. densiflorum*), or give rise to a single leaf as in the miniature *D. lindleyi*. Certain lines of cross breeding within the genus has proved successful, although only with those types which are closely related. It is fun to speculate that if all dendrobiums hybridised with each other, there would be some wildly imaginative specimens around!

Many dendrobiums are deciduous, losing their season's foliage during the winter and remaining dormant until the spring. The hybrids usually become evergreen under cultivation, as the harsh conditions prevailing in the wild are no longer encountered. Other species are evergreen or semi-deciduous, retaining their younger leaves for an additional season. The deciduous varieties have soft, paper-thin leaves, while the evergreen types have much firmer foliage, of a darker green. Dendrobiums produce the typical profusion of fine white roots, which are often made outside of the pot, reminiscent of their epiphytic origins. Many species, particularly the long-caned varieties, do well mounted on bark when their roots will extend downwards for up to a metre. Those dendrobiums which have leaves all along their canes will produce flowers in ones or twos from opposite the leaf bases, often after the leaves have been shed. A bare cane is transformed when blooming from tip to base, and the fragrant D. *anosum* with several canes in bloom at one time is a wondrous sight and scent. The harder-leafed types produce flower spikes from the upper half of the canes with numerous flowers clustered on hanging trusses (D. *densiflorum*) while others produce flower spikes carrying many flowers spread along the stem, (D. *bigibbum*).

While the Yamamoto hybrids have reached the pinnacle of success with their colourful beauty, there are others some of which are eccentric and even grotesque.

It is quite extraordinary that in a genus which has produced the very beautiful Yamamoto hybrids, there also appears species such as *Dendrobium stratiotes* whose eccentricity includes petals which arise, twisting above the flower, to resemble antelope horns; the vulgar flowers of D. *spectabile*, which can only be described as grotesque, and the equally strange D. *atroviolaceum* whose somewhat coarse flowers are among the most long-lived of all orchid blooms, lasting for six months or more. There are many more adaptations within this most exciting genus with surprises wherever you look, all of which makes dendrobiums worthy of more study or at the very least, comparison one with the other.

The majority of dendrobiums are cool growing, requiring a winter night temperature of 7°C or 10°C, with a significant rise during the day. This low night-time temperature suits these orchids which will be resting at this time and need as much light as possible

136. *Dendrobium miyakei.* A species from the Philippines with long, drooping canes, best grown either in a basket or on bark as a hanging plant.

137. *Dendrobium* Prima Donna. Continuing the theme of *D. nobile* hybridising, which gives an unlimited range of colours, shapes and sizes.

138. *Dendrobium nobile* var. *cooksonii*. A peloric form of *D. nobile* where the lip pattern has been repeated on the petals giving the impression of three lips. An unusual collectors' item which, when hybridised from, the peloria does not come through.

139 (Below). *Dendrobium* Super Star. One of the darker, more richly coloured hybrids from *D. nobile*.

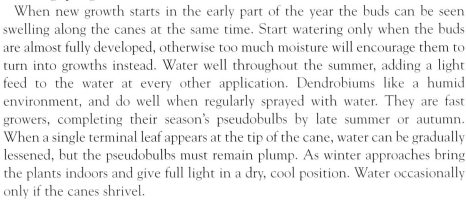

to ripen their long cane. Summer temperatures can rise to a daytime maximum of 30°C, provided there is sufficient moisture around to balance. Most dendrobiums will benefit from summering out of doors in a light area of dappled shade. Their growths will become noticeably shorter, stouter and yellowish, and they will bloom all the better the following spring.

When new growth starts in the early part of the year the buds can be seen swelling along the canes at the same time. Start watering only when the buds are almost fully developed, otherwise too much moisture will encourage them to turn into growths instead. Water well throughout the summer, adding a light feed to the water at every other application. Dendrobiums like a humid environment, and do well when regularly sprayed with water. They are fast growers, completing their season's pseudobulbs by late summer or autumn. When a single terminal leaf appears at the tip of the cane, water can be gradually lessened, but the pseudobulbs must remain plump. As winter approaches bring the plants indoors and give full light in a dry, cool position. Water occasionally only if the canes shrivel.

If you are growing some of the lesser well-known types from Papua New Guinea these need to be kept 5°C degrees warmer in winter, but otherwise the culture of the many varied kinds is basically the same. Slugs and snails are prone to eating the lush new growths when they first appear, and later Red Spider Mite

140. *Dendrobium farmeri*. This Indian species produces the most delicate pale-pink petals with a yellow lip. The intensity of colour varies with individual species.

141 (Above left). *Dendrobium brymerianum*. One of the most extraordinary dendrobiums with its huge golden-yellow, deeply frilled lip. This plant is easy to grow but is not always free-flowering.

142 (Above right). *Dendrobium* Hoshimusume. This is one of a huge range of hybrids raised from *D. nobile*. These are being produced in large quantities in Japan and Hawaii to meet the ever increasing pot-plant trade.

143 (Below left). *Dendrobium senile*. An unusual species from Thailand whose pseudobulbs are covered with protective short white hairs.

144 (Below right). *Dendrobium speciosum*. An Australian species producing long sprays of many blooms which are perfumed at certain times of the day.

145. *Dendrobium infundibulum*. A handsome, tall-growing species from the foothills of the Himalayas and the most striking of the white-flowered dendrobiums. The flowers are very long lasting, six to seven weeks in perfection being normal.

146. *Dendrobium densiflorum*. A most beautiful display of blooms is produced in large pendent clusters by this species from India. It is a very rewarding orchid to grow although the blooms only last seven to ten days.

147. *Dendrobium* Mousmee. A hybrid raised in the 1940s from *D. thyrsiflorum*. A most unusual, beautifully coloured flower, quite rare in cultivation and sought after by those who look for something different.

will attack the leaves of the softer types. Plenty of spraying with water will deter this latter pest at an early stage.

Repot immediately after flowering, using as small a pot as possible. The long-caned types will need supporting to prevent them from becoming top heavy. Take care not to bury the base of the plant which should sit on the surface of the compost to ensure that new growths starting at the base are not rotted off. Propagation often occurs naturally on some varieties when small adventitious growths form along the canes. Remove these when they have made their own roots and pseudobulb, and pot separately. These propagations will flower within two to three years. Where a quantity of new plants is required, an old leafless cane can be chopped up and the pieces placed in a pot to produce new growths. This method is usually only successful with the *D. nobile* types, and is not recommended for all dendrobiums.

148. *Dendrobium thyrsiflorum*. This species is related to *D. farmeri* and *D. densiflorum*. It has compact trusses of beautiful flowers which do not last very long. In spite of this, the plant is still well worth growing for its gorgeous displays.

Paphiopedilums

149. *Paphiopedilum villosum*. This species is slightly warmer-growing than *P. insigne* or *P. spicerianum*, but it is from the same group of Slipper Orchids, all of which come from the Himalayas.

These are the highly distinctive Slipper Orchids whose dramatic blooms with their characteristic pouch find many devotees. They are easily looked after and take up little room in a mixed collection. Hybrids are often available through garden centres and other outlets during their main winter flowering season, but a much wider choice can be found all year at the specialist nurseries.

Paphiopedilums produce leafy growths, without pseudobulbs, growing forward in the usual way, with each new growth starting from the base of the previous one. There may be from two, to several narrow leaves which vary in colour from mid-green to darker shades, sometimes tessellated on the upper surface, or peppered with purple underneath. The smallest of the species, such as *Paphiopedilum bellatulum*, have beautifully marbled, semi-rigid leaves, with a horizontal spread of less than 15cm. The single, 6cm wide bloom sits on a very short stem just 8cm high. While many species produce a single bloom on a stem which may reach 45cm high, as in *P. appletonianum*, others produce a multi-flowered spike which can be taller still (*parishii*). Undoubtedly, the most dramatic of the multi-flowered varieties is *P. rothschildianum*, a superb species from Borneo. In between these extremes are many highly desirable species, such as *P. insigne*, which have,

150 (Opposite). *Paphiopedilum insigne*. One of the earliest of the Slipper Orchids to be cultivated, it was once grown in huge numbers for the cut-flower market. It is a high altitude species from the Himalayas, which has been used extensively for hybridising and is in the background of modern, complex hybrids.

151 (Opposite). *Paphiopedilum* Leeanum. One of the first primary hybrids to be made between *P. insigne* and *P. spicerianum*, this old classic produces huge, long-lasting flowers. Not of modern shape, but very beautiful and interesting to grow.

152 (Right). *Paphiopedilum spicerianum*. Closely related to *P. insigne*, this species will readily interbreed with it and others to produce a variety of hybrids.

153 (Below left). *Paphiopedilum* Geelong. This is a complex hybrid, far removed from the original species where the pattern, dorsal and colour of petals is still retained down the generations.

154 (Below right). *Paphiopedilum* Jersey Freckles. This is another example of a complex hybrid with heavily-patterned long-lasting flowers.

over the last 150 years, produced a multitude of splendid hybrids, extending the colour range through powdery white and pink, to deep golden-yellow, through copper and bronze shades to rich mahogany reds, all with a waxed, glossy texture not found in any other orchids. These numerous hybrids are known collectively as the complex or green-leafed hybrids, and some of their blooms are extremely large and heavy, of a very rounded appearance. A second type which complements the former, are known as the mottled-leafed, or vini-coloured hybrids, and these have come about from such handsome species as *P. callosum*. Many years of breeding with these lighter, more open shaped flowers have assembled a race of clear, spring-green varieties with striped dorsals, as well as superbly brooding rich purples, the darkest of which border on black. Further imposing hybrids have widened this range until all tastes are catered for.

Paphiopedilums produce their flower spikes from the centre of the newest growth.

155 (Above left). *Paphiopedilum* Atlantis. This is an example of the more heavily marked, rather than daintily spotted, complex hybrids.

156 (Above right). *Paphiopedilum* Jac Flash. This is the same line of breeding as *P.* Gothic Garden, only here the vini-colour form has been used to produce the rich, wine-red flowers. All this group have interesting mottled leaves.

157 (Left). *Paphiopedilum* Gothic Garden. These pure-green-on-a-white-ground slipper orchids have never been out of fashion and there is a group of them worth collecting. Blooming for four to five months, they are among the longest lasting flowers.

158. *Paphiopedilum* Gina Short. This pink hybrid, seen here with three flowers on one stem, is a very attractive and long-lasting variety. The plant has well-mottled foliage.

159. *Paphiopedilum* Golddollar. This is one of an exciting breed of modern hybrids from the recently discovered Chinese species. In many cases the hybrids are not of a higher quality or as attractive as the species.

Naturally drooping, the flowers need to be tied back after fully opening to be seen at their best. The complex varieties tend to be mostly winter blooming, while the vini-coloured types and others will give their flowers during the summer, or at various other times. They produce a rather sparse root system with short roots that are brown and hairy.

All the flowers are extremely long lasting and will remain on the plant for ten weeks or so. Those which have sequential flowering will produce a continuous succession of blooms over many months before the flower spike eventually dies, by which time the next one will be flowering, and in this way the plant becomes perpetual blooming. Numerous hybrids of this sort have been raised from *Paphiopedilum glaucophyllum* and other closely related species.

While many orchids have benefitted from cloning by meristem culture, to date paphiopedilums have resisted all attempts to encourage them to propagate in this way. This means that you will be buying a seedling, which will vary slightly from others of the same cross. It is a good idea to select plants in bloom to be sure of getting the colour and shape which appeals to you the most.

While a number of *Paphiopedilum* species are cool growing, most are for the intermediate range, and the hybrids raised from them certainly benefit from being grown at a winter night temperature of 13°C, with the appropriate rise during the day. In summer the temperature range can extend up to 26°C, and indoor culture suits them

160. *Paphiopedilum* Rosy Dawn. This is one of the oldest of the white hybrids. It is still popular today for its ease of culture and willingness to bloom.

well. They are shade-loving plants, which are not suitable for summering out of doors. They prefer a comfortable and shady area indoors or in a greenhouse which is well controlled. Exposure to too much direct sunlight will scorch their fleshy leaves and quickly lead to dehydration.

Paphiopedilums do not have a resting period, they are mainly terrestrial plants, occasionally epiphytic, which like to be evenly moist at their roots throughout the year. They cannot stand long periods of drought, and will quickly succumb to rot if kept in a sodden state for any length of time. Do not spray the leaves with water as this can run down into the centre of the growths and cause rotting there. Feeding can be light and all year round, giving less in winter when the light is poor and temperatures low. There are very few insect pests which will attack the relatively tough leaves of the paphiopedilums, but false Red Spider Mite can cause pitting to the leaf surface and where this is seen, clean the leaves with methylated spirits before washing off with tepid water, or use a recommended insecticide.

Keep these orchids in as small a pot as possible, the plant will seldom become rootbound, and will often return to the same size pot after having the old compost and dead roots removed. Propagation is not really successful, and it is far better to keep a plant intact with several growths combining to present a strong plant capable of producing several flowers at one time. Repot in the spring unless buds are showing, in

161. *Paphiopedilum* Prime Child. A primary hybrid from *P. rothchildianum* and *P. primulinum* which gives three to four flowers on a stem. These large blooms, with their long tapering petals, are highly sought after by collectors.

which case repot after flowering. Paphiopedilums are well suited to the modern Rockwool type material which can be kept evenly moist without the fear of rotting the plant. Otherwise, use an open bark mix of a coarse grade. Take care to ensure that the plant is firm in its pot after repotting. If potted too high or if insecure, repeat the process, placing the plant slightly lower in the compost.

Hybrids far outweigh the number of species grown, and many of the latter are now

162. *Paphiopedilum* Avalon Mist. This is a sequential-flowering hybrid (as soon as a flower dies another one appears on the same stem) capable of producing six, seven or more flowers on a large plant over a long period.

extremely rare or endangered in their natural habitats. The species come from a wide area stretching from India and China down through the Philippines and Indonesia to Papua New Guinea. All are on the CITES Appendix 1 which protects them from being traded. In view of the wonderfully spectacular hybrids which have been raised, there really is no excuse for pillaging the wild colonies where they still exist and which are only hankered after by the over zealous collector.

Phalaenopsis and Doritaenopsis

163. *Phalaenopsis* Cool Breeze. This is a typical, modern white hybrid with a distinctive yellow lip grown for the pot-plant trade.

Phalaenopsis and their close relatives the doritis will readily interbreed to produce the equally popular, man-made genus, *Doritaenopsis*. Through breeding the two have become indistinguishable, apart from the rich colouring which has been added to the doritaenopsis. The two natural genera comprise a large part of another horticultural family headed by the vandas, and these two groups have been interbred with many of their associated genera to give rise to an ever expanding number of artificial hybrids which has extended the choice a hundred fold. The majority of these intergeneric crosses are grown in the tropics where these plants thrive. In the northern hemisphere it is the phalaenopsis and doritaenopsis which grow and flower best, and for indoor culture, they are second to none. Plants in bloom appear regularly in garden centres, while a wider selection can be found all year round in the specialist nurseries.

These orchids are short-growing monopodials, with broad fleshy leaves which are produced from the centre of a vertical rhizome. The plants are self-regulating never retaining more than five or six leaves at any time. The old leaves are shed at the rate of one or two per year from the base, where the roots develop. These roots are thick, flattened, and silvery white with a pink or green growing tip. They are often reluctant to grow into the pot, but will extend over the edge and progress along any surface or hang suspended in air. They will adhere to whatever surface they come into contact with, which can make problems for the grower when the plants need to be moved.

164. *Phalaenopsis* Miva
Barbara x *P*. Colombiana.
A white flower crossed
with a yellow has
produced a creamy-
yellow, delicate hybrid.

These aerial roots are more likely to be made under greenhouse cultivation where there is more moisture to encourage them out of the pot. In nature the plants are epiphytic, their strong roots hold them firmly onto their host trees, and in this situation the plants often assume a downward habit.

The flower spikes appear from the base of a mature leaf, and it is not unusual for phalaenopsis to bloom two to three times a year. The long-stemmed, large-flowered types are unique among the cultivated orchids in that you can cut back the spike when the first flowers have finished, and more often than not it will branch out again to give an extended flowering season. In this way large plants can become forever blooming. The tall spikes will require the support of a thin bamboo cane to keep them upright. There can be up to two dozen blooms on a spike, although eight or ten are more usual. The most popular varieties come in a host of shades starting with clear pristine white, through many shades of warm pink to the glowing mauves and clear canary yellows. These softly rounded flowers with wide generous petals can be self-coloured with

165. *Phalaenopsis* Golden Hat. This type of yellow is popular because of the red peppering around the centre of the flower.

166. *Phalaenopsis* Yellow Treasure. Some of the early yellow hybrids were quick to fade to cream, but modern hybrids such as this hold their colour well, providing they are kept out of the full sun.

167. *Phalaenopsis* Golden Bells. This line of breeding produces fewer flowers per spike, but the flowers are longer lasting. The stem is smaller and more compact than the long-spiked varieties.

contrasting lips, or spotted or striped in a multitude of pretty variations. All have sprays of large, attractive flowers 5cm to 8cm across, of a delicate nature, which has earned them their common name of Moth Orchids. The lip is small and curiously shaped in some hybrids. This is by far the largest group of desirable *Phalaenopsis*. Adding further variety are numerous additional hybrids bred from distinct sections of the genus which have created smaller plants with more compact sprays of blooms, and others again which exhibit wide open, starry flowers on shorter stems. There is so much variance from more specialised multigeneric hybrids within the family, it is hard to keep pace with the stream of new varieties coming along.

The culture of *Phalaenopsis* and *Doritaenopsis* is surprisingly easy. They succeed well in a warm greenhouse given plenty of shade, and also do remarkably well indoors where they are kept out of direct sunlight. They will live permanently in the centre of a room where other orchids would find insufficient light. Their temperature range is within 18°C to 30°C, with a considerable variation between day and night, summer and winter. Although they like to be warm, do not be tempted to place phalaenopsis in an unsuitable area such as above a heat source, where a direct current of warm air impinging upon the leaves will quickly cause dehydration and eventual death.

168. *Phalaenopsis* Lady Sakara. One of the modern candy-striped varieties with a dark lip, where the striping will vary from one cross to another, making each an individual.

169. *Phalaenopsis* Pinlong Diana. A different line of breeding has created a shining flower of harder appearance, making it longer lasting.

170. *Phalaenopsis* Petite Snow. This dainty hybrid has been bred from the species *P. equestris* to give branching flower spikes and a multi-flowering habit that will last for many months.

171 (Above). *Phalaenopsis* Little Mary. A compact, multi-flowering, easy-to-grow hybrid which produces a succession of flowers enabling it to last perfectly for many months.

172. *Phalaenopsis* Purple Valley. One of the darkest hybrids produced to date, this has a perfectly shaped bloom with a dark lip.

173. *Doritaenopsis* Rendezvous. This is another of the dark-pink varieties with this one showing a touch of candy stripe through the petals.

174. *Phalaenopsis* Spanish Melody. A darker, and more heavily-marked hybrid than usual, with a white margin to the petals, which contribute to an outstanding flower.

175. *Doritaenopsis* Quevedo. This modern hybrid has a branching flower spike with numerous small flowers sporting highly coloured lips.

Water phalaenopsis all year round, avoiding the extremes of getting the plants overwet or bone dry at any time. Do not spray the leaves, because of the danger of water lodging in the crown, which can easily cause rot. Feeding can be given all year, but less in winter when you can reduce the feed from every other watering to every third watering. Indoors, wipe the leaves occasionally with a wet paper tissue to remove dust and dirt. Take care when handling these orchids, their leaves are semi-rigid and can be easily snapped or damaged. This also applies to their roots, which need to be treated with care where they are growing outside of the pot. Phalaenopsis will remain healthy with the minimum of care, but watch out for a pitting on the leaf surfaces which may indicate an attack from false Red Spider Mite. Too small to be seen clearly, it is the damage which results from the pest puncturing the leaf which is visible. This will also cause premature leaf shedding and weaken the plant. Other ailments which are brought about by cold and damp are watery patches on the leaves, which is some cases can spread

176. *Doritaenopsis*
Kiska. Here, hybridising
has been taken to such
an extreme there is
hardly any *Doritis*
visible. The main
feature of the flower is
its pure white petals
and orange lip.

throughout the whole leaf. Any affected parts can be cut away, and the exposed edge dusted with sulphur to dry up the wound. Limp foliage will be the result of over or under watering. Tap the plant out of its pot to determine which is the cause, and if necessary repot. Mist the foliage lightly to prevent further dehydration.

Phalaenopsis and doritaenopsis do well in a Rockwool type of compost, where it becomes easier to keep them moist at all times, with less danger of overwatering and causing the roots to rot. If grown in a bark mix, use a coarse grade and keep the plants slightly dryer, especially in the winter. These orchids will not fill their pot in the same way as those with a sympodial growth, but will need regular repotting to remove the old, decaying compost and have it replaced with new. Often the plants will return to the same size, or a slightly larger pot. Plants growing in Rockwool need to be repotted less often as the medium will not decay. Aerial roots should be allowed to remain outside of the pot, to tuck them inside the compost will suffocate them. Compare the different structures of the roots inside and outside the pot. Because phalaenopsis spend so much of their time producing flowers, repot when you can after flowering, but avoid disturbing the plants during the shortest days of winter. Propagation is difficult and not recommended, but new plants will occasionally grow from old flowering stems on some types. Plants will also grow from the base where the centre has been damaged.

The multitude of hybrids are the first choice for the hobby grower. The species from which they have been raised belong to the specialist collector, and these occur throughout the Old World, from India, parts of Asia, down through Indonesia, the Philippines and into Northern Australia. This wide distribution has led to vast differences between the species, which fall into five distinct groups. All have been interbred, along with the many other genera to which these lovely orchids are related.

177. *Doritaenopsis* Aposya. This is a hybrid from *Phalaenopsis* and *Doritis*. The *Doritis* has given the flower the heavy, dark pigmentation, and a long lasting quality.

Vandas and related genera

Vandas are a genus of spectacularly gorgeous orchids presiding over an extended family of related genera with which they have interbred to produce a myriad of multigeneric hybrids. Most of these are best suited to the warmer parts of the world where there is good light all the year round. In the Northern hemisphere there is a limited choice of suitable hybrids, which are extremely variable, and which need to be looked out for in the specialist nurseries. To do this is to enter the realms of the fabled blue orchids, one colour among many, which this genus has made its own creation.

Vandas are medium to tall growing plants, producing their semi-rigid long and narrow, mid-green leaves in alternate pairs from an ever lengthening upright stem which provide a fan-like appearance. In time, as the plants extend upward and older leaves from the base are shed, the plants become 'leggy' with a length of bare stem from which white, stiffened aerial roots will grow and extend for up to a metre on some plants. This is a typical monopodial habit, with the flower spikes being produced at the base of the leaves. Up to six large, flat and well rounded blooms 5-6cm across, are produced with the characteristically huge sepals. Their colours almost defy description, but pale to dark blues, mauves, amazing lustrous reds and browns are predominant, each colour washed across the sepals as if laid on by an artist's brush and tessellated, mottled or veined overall, in combinations of colour not found in any other orchids.

The culture of *Vanda* type hybrids varies considerably depending upon the breeding behind the plant. Some are cool growing, and become extremely free flowering, while others require more warmth and humidity with all year round sunshine. It is necessary, therefore, to select with care those hybrids which will do well in the conditions you can provide for your other orchids. Outstanding among the hybrids is the deep blue *Vanda* Rothschildiana, which will grow fairly cool and flower freely along with other crosses made with the species *Vanda coerulea*. Another successful species used to produce cool growing hybrids is *Vanda (Trudelia) cristata*, a delightful, more compact growing plant which produces narrow-petalled green flowers with a richly red decorated white lip. This, and a few other species can be found in cultivation, and are well worth growing alongside the larger, more flamboyant types. A further genus with which the vandas will readily interbreed to produce smaller flowered, but richly coloured varieties, is *Ascocentrum*, and the resulting ascocendas are totally irresistible and much in demand for their vibrant hues.

Most of the vandas and their allies are best suitable to a greenhouse, where their love of fresh air and humidity can be more easily catered for. Most need a temperature range of between 11°C and 30°C, with humidity and temperatures always in balance. Give these orchids plenty of light, but keep them out of the direct sun. A good place to grow them is suspended from the greenhouse roof, when their copious aerial roots can remain

178 (Opposite). *Ascocenda* Crownfox Sunshine x A. Rainbow. Here a different line of breeding has been followed to give the typical, small, brightly coloured *Ascocenda hybrid*.

179. *Vanda* Fuchs Beauty. There are many excellent vandas producing large, showy patterned flowers which are at their best when grown in tropical conditions. They will adapt well, however, to growing in cooler climates in a tropical greenhouse.

180. *Vanda* Kitty Blue. Another excellent hybrid showing the tessellated patterns which are inherited from the species *Vanda coerulea*. It is a high-altitude, cool growing plant from Burma.

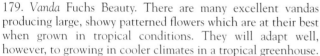

suspended in air. Spray regularly, several times daily in summer, to maintain moisture, and apply a foliar feed at every other watering, but keep much drier in winter. Avoid getting water on the flower spikes or open blooms. The plants will produce flowers intermittently, several times throughout the year. There are not many pests which will tolerate the constant spraying of water on the foliage, but aphids coming into the greenhouse from outside can build up unseen on the flower spikes, and need to be watched out for.

Vandas do best when grown in open slatted baskets of a small size. They require very little in the way of compost around their roots, and can be grown quite well with no compost whatsoever. In countries such as Thailand where they are raised from seed the young plants are attached to lumps of charcoal and placed in baskets. Within a short

181 (Opposite). *Ascocenda* David Peterson x *Rhynchostylis coelestis*. This orchid should be grown as tropical vandas. Its upright flower spikes and intense colouring make it a real collectors' item.

182 (Above). *Ascocenda* Crownfox Sunshine. This beautiful, perfectly shaped, delicate yellow flower shows signs of green in the colouring. It is only a matter of time before similar new colours continue to appear.

183 (Right). *Ascocenda* Vernon Kebodeaux. As a result of much line breeding there is little *Ascocentrum* left in this hybrid. With its beautiful, large, flat flowers and delicate colouring it is a most attractive orchid.

184 (Opposite). *Vascostylis* Five Friendships 'Sweetheart'. This is an inter-generic hybrid between *Ascocentrum*, *Rhynchostylis* and *Vanda* producing flowers on upright spikes. Grow this attractive orchid in the tropical *Vanda* house where its long-lasting blooms make a good contrast with conventional vandas.

time their strong aerial roots have anchored the plants to their containers. However, filling the basket with large pieces of bark chippings can help to retain extra moisture around the roots. Propagation, as with most monopodial orchids is not generally attempted, but a plant whose crown has become damaged will often produce new growths from lower down on the stem.

Most *Vanda* species are plants for the specialist while some are rare in cultivation. Their natural habitat range is epiphytic throughout India and Burma, parts of Asia (including Indio-China), spreading down through the Philippine Islands to New Guinea and parts of Australia. A similar area is covered by the much smaller genus *Ascocentrum*.

---

185 (Above). *Doricentrum* Pulcherrimin. A close-up of the flower showing the intricate detail of the colouring and shape. This orchid grows well in the *Phalaenopsis* house.

186 (Opposite). *Doricentrum* Pulcherrimin. This small, compact-growing plant with pretty, upright flower spikes is a bi-generic hybrid between *Doritis pulcherrima* and *Ascocentrum miniatum*.

Coelogynes

Ease of growing, a willingness to bloom freely with an abundance of starry-eyed flowers and the compact size of many of the Indian *Coelogyne* species, elevates them to the top position for a beginner's choice. This is a genus which has few hybrids to offer, but contains some delightful species, many of which are easily propagated commercially and are available from specialist nurseries.

Coelogynes vary greatly in their size, from the smaller species with pseudobulbs 2cm tall, as in *Coelogyne fimbriata*, to the largest with pseudobulbs reaching 10cm high, (*C. elata*). Mostly the pseudobulbs are green and shiny, in some species (*C. ochracea*) resembling large grapes. Each pseudobulb supports two short or long, narrow or oval leaves. Their roots are often brownish, sparsely produced and short. The flowers come

188 (Opposite). *Coelogyne cristata*. An ideal beginners' orchid, but not everyone finds it easy to flower. The secret of success is lots of water during the summer growing season to encourage large, fat pseudobulbs from which the flower spikes will come.

189. *Coelogyne flavida*. A small-flowered species with a trailing growth habit, and flower spikes which will produce a succession of small blooms over several years.

190. *Coelogyne flavida*. Close-up of the small, bright canary yellow flowers. This species comes from India.

either from the new growth when it is very young (C. *ochracea*), or from the base of the completed pseudobulb (C. *cristata*), or from the centre of the season's mature pseudobulb (C. *fimbriata*). The flower spikes may be short or long, single or multi-flowered. In some species (C. *flavida*), the same flower spike will produce blooms over several seasons while others, such as C. *massangeana*, produce their flowers on tumbling vertical spikes. Some, like C. *ochracea* are deliciously scented.

The coelogynes bloom in the spring, many having comparatively large flowers for

their small size. The main colours range from shining white, through buff and light brown shades to fresh greens. Some have highly coloured lips, which contrast well with the equally sized sepals and petals. It is very unusual among orchids to find flowers without a hint of any other colour or lip ornamentation. *Coelogyne cristata* var. *alba* is one of a small number of elite varieties which has no other colour than white. A large plant in bloom will almost completely disappear under a frothing deluge of rippling flowers which will transform it for weeks throughout the spring.

The coelogynes divide into both cool and intermediate varieties. The temperature range for the cool growing types, which include all those from the Indian continent, is 10°C in winter, to 30°C in summer. Within this limitation, there can be considerable differences between day and night, summer and winter temperatures. The intermediate coelogynes are the larger species from Malaysia and for these plants to grow well they require a minimum temperature of 13°C, with a greater rise during winter days. Many of the cool growing coelogynes will do extremely well summering out of doors.

Coelogynes are evergreen epiphytes, used to a regime of monsoon rains followed by a

191. *Coelogyne lawrenceana.* A tall-growing plant which carries large blooms with striking white lips. The deep flame-red throat makes an attractive honey guide for the insect pollinator.

192. *Coelogyne mooreana* 'Brockhurst' FCC/RHS. This is one of the most beautiful of all the coelogynes, known originally from a limited importation from Vietnam at the beginning of the twentieth century. The huge, glistening white flowers make it a highly collectable orchid.

193. *Coelogyne speciosa*. An unusual *Coelogyne* where the petals are reduced to ribbon-like strips which are hidden behind the flower. A huge lip dominates the flower and when one bloom has finished another will open on the flower spike.

194. *Coelogyne ochracea*. One of the most beautiful of the miniature coelogynes, found at high altitudes in the Himalayas. It is cool growing, free-flowering and has a strong perfume while in bloom.

dry season. In cultivation they like an almost completely dry resting period which commences in late autumn, after the pseudobulbs have matured, and continues until the new growth can be seen to be on the move in early spring. During this time the plants will only need watering if the pseudobulbs begin to shrivel badly. Some slight shrivelling is inevitable and is natural at this time. Keep the plants in full light for the winter which will encourage the new growths to flower, most of them doing this when the new growth is still very young. After flowering, water and feed on a regular basis to keep the compost evenly moist. Some shade will be necessary from the spring onwards to prevent burning of the leaves. Regular spraying or misting of the leaves is also beneficial during the summer while the plants are active, but avoid getting water on to the flowers which will cause them to spot and not last so long. Grow coelogynes in an open type of compost which is swift draining. They do well in pots or hanging baskets where they can be left to become quite large and be seen at their best.

196. *Coelogyne* Green Dragon 'Chelsea' AM/RHS (*C. massangeana* x *C. pandurata*). A fascinating, modern hybrid which flowers freely and produces long, pendent flower spikes of richly coloured flowers. The dark, almost black lip, comes from the species *C. pandurata*.

195 (Above). *Coelogyne rochussenii*. This is one of a group which are best grown in baskets to accommodate their long, thin pendent flower spikes which are produced in summer.

197. *Coelogyne* Memoria William Micholitz 'Burnham' AM/RHS. This is a striking hybrid from *C. lawrenceana* and *C. mooreana* which has inherited the best of both parents.

198. *Coelogyne* Brymeriana. A hybrid between two Malaysian species, C. *asperata* and C. *dayana*, raised by Revd. Brymer in Dorchester, England. A rare and unusual hybrid.

Coelogynes keep comparatively free from most insect pests, but where conditions are dry and warm, keep an eye out for Red Spider Mite. These orchids can be easily propagated by division or removal of the leafless backbulbs, but where they are allowed to grow on undisturbed the rewards are even greater.

The species originate from India, China and down through the Philippines and Indonesia. The smaller growing species such as C. *cristata*, and C. *fimbriata* are ideal for window-sill culture where no suitable greenhouse is available. C. *ochracea* is a bit more of a challenge and needs to be cool and dry in winter during its rest. In spring this orchid rewards with highly scented, prettily decorated, white-petalled flowers.

Encyclias and epidendrums

199. *Encyclia brassavolae.* One of the largest-growing of the encyclias capable of producing big specimen plants with a huge display of blooms.

Within these two closely related genera can be found plants which are either extremely small or tall and leggy. In between are a number of highly desirable species, which are renowned for their pretty, fragrant blooms on modestly sized plants which are a joy to grow. There are very few notable hybrids here, and it is the more colourful and attractive species which have found great favour with hobbyists. These plants are frequently found in the specialist nurseries, but are unlikely to appear in other outlets.

Encyclias are evergreen epiphytes coming mostly from Mexico and parts of the West Indies. Many of them are strikingly similar, and typically produce elongated, pencil-length pseudobulbs which carry a pair of mid-green, narrowly-oval leaves. The roots can be abundant, following the growth of the new pseudobulbs in the spring. The flowers are produced from between the leaves at the apex of the pseudobulb. Often the flower spikes are short, with from two to many flowers. Typically, these are held with their lip at the top of the flower and many are creamy white with a red veined lip such as *Encyclia radiata* and *E. lancifolia*. Others have more rounded, cone-shaped pseudobulbs, with longer leaves and taller flower spikes producing flowers of a waxy or firmer texture, the sepals and petals well spaced apart, and the lip on the lower plane as in *E. nemorale*.

200 (Opposite). *Encyclia radiata.* This highly-fragrant, summer flowering species from Honduras and Mexico makes a large specimen plant very easily.

201. *Encyclia chondylobulbon*. A species from Mexico which flowers in the summer and carries a strong perfume.

202. *Encyclia lancifolia*. Another species from the same group as *E. chondylobulbon* and *E. radiata*. It is summer flowering and well perfumed.

203. *Encyclia nemorale*. This species produces long, slender flower spikes with large heads of pale pink to dark rose blooms.

204 (Opposite). *Encyclia radiata*. Close up of the flowers showing how the lip is held uppermost. These blooms will last from six to eight weeks.

Further types show extreme variations, so that a very diverse group of plants emerge after all. One of the showiest is *E. vitellina*, which is the only red-flowered member of the genus, while *E. citrina*, which is seen less often now, produces large, pendent citron-yellow, fragrant blooms. Most of the encyclias are suitable for indoor culture, the smaller varieties especially so. They can be maintained at a manageable size by regular division, or they can be grown on to specimen size. A number of them are particularly suited to basket culture, where they can remain for several years without disturbance.

205. *Encyclia vitellina.* An unusual *Encyclia* with bright orange-red blooms, it lacks the perfume and stamina of some of the others.

Encyclias are cool growing orchids, so are content with the temperatures at the lower end of the scale. During the winter these should not drop below 10°C at night, with an increase during the day which can rise to a summer maximum of 30°C. Within this range a daily variation is necessary as weather and seasons change. In a greenhouse they respond well to a cool environment where they require shade during the summer and full light in the winter. Encyclias can be watered well throughout the summer months, following the start of their new growth in the spring. They bloom mainly in early summer as the growths mature into pseudobulbs. As winter approaches watering and feeding is reduced, and almost stopped during the coldest, shortest days. The advent of early spring sees the cycle repeated once again.

Encyclias and epidendrums remain comparatively free from most insect pests, and where good culture prevails there is little to harm them. During the summer growing season light overhead spraying of the leaves is beneficial, but take care not to get the plants or their pots too wet for a prolonged period, because this may result in damp spots on the leaves, showing up as ugly black patches, or basal rot where the compost has become sodden. For this reason they are best

206. *Epidendrum ilense.* A rare, and fairly recent discovery from Costa Rica. The white flowers with frilled lips bloom freely on any sized plants. Because it can be raised easily from seed, there are now more plants in cultivation than in the wild.

207. *Epicattleya* Siam Jade. A miniature, easy-to-grow plant prized for its beautiful, green and yellow petals with a pure white lip. This is a hybrid between *Epidendrum (Encyclia)* and *Cattleya*.

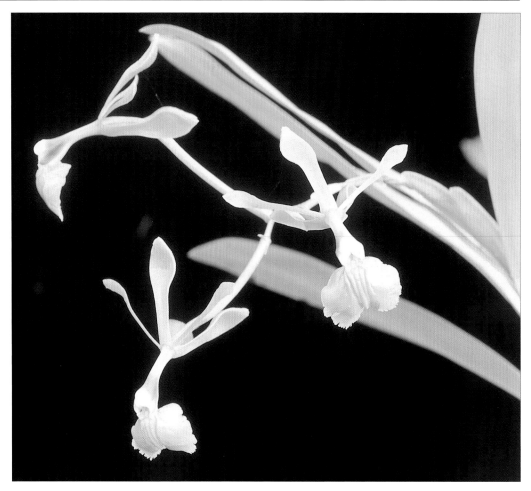

208. *Epidendrum pseudepidendrum*. One of the tall, reed-type epidendrums. Some varieties have the red lip, whilst others have the yellow lip. It becomes almost continuously flowering, and makes an ideal plant of the cool to intermediate greenhouse.

grown indoors throughout the year, unless a really sheltered place out of doors can be found for them in summer.

Repotting is needed about every two to three years, and division and propagation is easy for many of them. *E. vitellina* is slower growing and needs a little more care. It will rarely divide, although leafless back bulbs will, when removed and potted up, produce new growths in a short time.

Among the epidendrums are several tall growing, reed-type species, and a few primary hybrids which have been made between them. These plants are distinct from the encyclias by their growth, which lightly resembles bamboo. From the top of long, leafy canes the flower spikes emerge to produce a cluster of blooms which can be considerably varied, but with red, orange and yellow flowers found. *Epidendrum pseudepidendrum* is a particularly colourful species, with flowers that appear almost plastic and highly coloured with narrow, green sepals and petals and an amazing bright orange lip. At the other end of the scale can be found the diminutive pixie-like *E. porpax*, a delightful, miniature creeping plant with glistening round pseudobulbs and flowers, large for the size of the plant, which are brown to green, with a waxy brown, convex lip. The miniature epidendrums can be grown alongside the cool encyclias, some of which they closely resemble in stature. The taller epidendrums need plenty of headroom to be grown well, and are at their best placed at one end of the intermediate greenhouse with temperatures as for the cattleyas. They like good light all year, with the minimum of shade during the summer. Water and feed regularly during the summer, and give less of both during the winter when the plants need to be kept just moist, but on the dry side until new growth is seen in the spring.

When repotting these tall-growing epidendrums, it is tempting to overpot to reduce the danger of their becoming top heavy. Keep them in as small a pot as possible, as their surface width is quite small. After potting, support the plants with a cane, and if necessary, place the pot in a larger container to prevent it from falling over. One distinct group which contains the species *E. imatophyllum* and *E. radicans*, produces canes which will extend over several years before reaching maturity and flowering. These types readily produce new adventitious growths from the old flowering stems. These can be potted up at almost any time once roots are made, and grown on. If you have the space in a cool or intermediate greenhouse, plant them out in a ground-level bed made up with a compost of bark chippings, and they can remain in the same position for years without any further disturbance and with the minimum of attention. When large enough, these plants will become perpetually flowering with individual flowering heads lasting for many months and a succession of buds maintaining the process. These wonderfully showy orchids are often under-rated or not grown on to their full regal size to be appreciated as they should.

Epidendrums come from a wide area throughout Central and South America.

209. *Epidendrum porpax*. A miniature *Epidendrum* species making small compact plants suitable for growing in a pan or mounted on bark.

Angraecums

Here is a superb genus of dramatic, mostly white-flowered orchids which could lay claim to be the prize possessions of the Ice Maiden, so crisp and clear cut are their flowers they could have been chipped from ice. A few species and less hybrids are found in the collections of enthusiasts who covert them. They have to be searched out from the corners of commercial specialist nurseries. Their comparative rarity in cultivation reflects their protected status in the wild.

Angraecums are evergreen, monopodial-type orchids which vary greatly in size from a few centimetres high to over a metre. They produce a vanda-type growth with leaves growing from the tip of an ever extending stem. The leaves may be small, terete or wide and strap-like. Thick aerial roots are a feature of these plants which, in good conditions, will become numerous and robust. The flowers are produced from flower spikes which appear at the base of the older leaves. They may be one, two or many flowered. These can be really tiny, (half a centimetre in *Angraecum distichum*, a diminutive species with 'plaited' overlapping foliage), to very large (12cm across in *A. sesquipedale*). All carry a distinctive spur, which is an extension of the base of the lip. The spur contains nectar at its base, and in some species can be extremely long. *A. sesquipedale*, commonly known as the Comet Orchid because of its white, symmetrical, star-shaped chiselled flowers, has a spur about 30cm long. Its long white lip is pointed as melting ice. Its name translates to 'a-foot-and-a-half' which is a little exaggeration. The angraecums are pollinated by night-flying moths, hence the flowers are mostly large and white. A few of them are also fragrant during the hours of darkness.

The thick-rooted species grow in a compost of coarse bark chunks, to which can be added a little chopped *Sphagnum* moss. Good drainage is essential and they need to be evenly watered throughout the year, allowing the plants to partially dry out in between waterings. Feeding can be light all year, given at every other watering. The smaller growing varieties often do well when mounted, and some grow downward making pot culture difficult. Like the majority of monopodial orchids, they do not propagate readily and will only produce secondary growths from near their base if the centre of the plant is damaged and unable to grow normally.

The angraecums are warm house orchids, and do best when grown in the same conditions as the phalaenopsis, but with more light. Ideally, they need a minimum temperature of 18°C, rising by day to 30°C. When the temperature is high, there should be a high humidity to balance. The smaller plants growing on bark need regular spraying, but keep all moisture away from the waxy blooms. These will usually last for up to three

210 (Opposite). *Angraecum sesquipedale*. A magnificent species from Madagascar with an unusually long spur at the back of the flower in which the nectar, to tempt the night-flying moth, is found.

220. *Angraecum* Veitchii. Showing the twisted ovary at the back of the flower. The bloom turns as it gradually develops before opening.

221 (Opposite). *Angraecum* Veitchii. This is a hybrid of A. *sesquipedale*. The other parent A. *eburneum*, is from the African mainland and holds its flowers lip uppermost. The hybrid holds its blooms sideways to the stem.

weeks, but can easily become bruised or spotted through over-damp conditions. The angraecums bloom mostly during the winter.

The species come mainly from Madagascar and East Africa. They are closely related to *Aerangis* which are sometimes easier to find in cultivation.

The toughened foliage of angraecums renders them fairly safe from most insect pests. Red Spider Mite or scale insects will only get a hold on these plants where conditions are on the warm and dry side without sufficient humidity. Because their leaves will live for a good number of years, as they age, the older ones can become spotted or marked. If the whole plant is affected this is usually an indication of cold or over wet conditions, otherwise, there is little to worry about.

Adas, aspasias, brassias and barkerias

222. Aspasia lunata.
A species from Brazil, easily grown in the intermediate house where it will quickly make a specimen plant. The star-shaped flowers are borne singly but on a good specimen there will be several flower spikes.

These orchids have been placed together for convenience and because they are compatible with each other, requiring the same growing conditions. They form a single grouping yet give variety of flower. The adas, aspasias and brassias are related to the *Odontoglossum* family and will interbreed with them and other members of this alliance. Barkerias are botanically separate. These orchids are for the enthusiast and can usually be found in the collections of the serious grower alongside many other colourful and interesting species.

Adas, aspasias and brassias produce plants resembling odontoglossums. The barkerias produce slender, cane-like stems, and are the only ones in this group which are deciduous and need a dry winter's rest.

Ada aurantiaca produces compact arching spikes of closely-set, bright orange, tubular flowers in early summer. It originates from Colombia but is no longer taken from the wild. The plants in cultivation have been nursery propagated. One or two other *Ada* species, and occasionally intergeneric hybrids are also grown.

Aspasia lunata grows along a creeping rhizome, its slender pseudobulbs spread out across the pot surface. It blooms in the early summer and produces a single flower on a short stem from the base. The idyllically star-shaped bloom, 3cm across, has narrow sepals and petals, green spotted with brown. The white lip has a hint of mauve at the centre. This species propagates easily thus ensuring its continuance in cultivation. One or two other *Aspasia* species are also occasionally grown.

223. *Ada aurantiaca*. This beautiful high altitude, fairly cool growing species comes from Colombia. It is related to odontoglossums and brassias with which it will interbreed. Most hybrids have been unsuccessful in keeping the bright orange colour, though this may be the fault of the hybridiser. There could be a good future for this orchid in the right hands.

Brassia verrucosa is one of several species known as Spider Orchids, for their extremely long and narrow sepals and petals. This species is most often found in cultivation along with a few outstanding hybrids. *B. verrucosa* flowers in early summer producing tall flower spikes with up to a dozen fragrant, spidery blooms which are 12cm long, light green dotted with a darker colour. The lip is white, dotted with darker green.

Barkeria spectabilis is the showiest of several attractive species and produces its flowers from an extended stem which is the continuation of the leafed cane. The plant will often bloom after the leaves have been shed when the upright stem can carry up to a dozen pale pink flowers, their pretty lips decorated with a few reddish spots. Other varieties which are worth looking out for are *B. skinneri*, which has deep rosy-pink flowers, and *B. lindleyana*, which has paler blooms.

224. *Brassia* Rex. A hybrid between *B. verrucosa* x *gireoudiana*, Rex is one of the most popular in the genus because of its extremely large, showy blooms and willingness to flower.

225. *Brassia verrucosa.* A species from Mexico and Guatemala which flowers in the early summer and produces large, slender-petalled blooms, with a strong perfume.

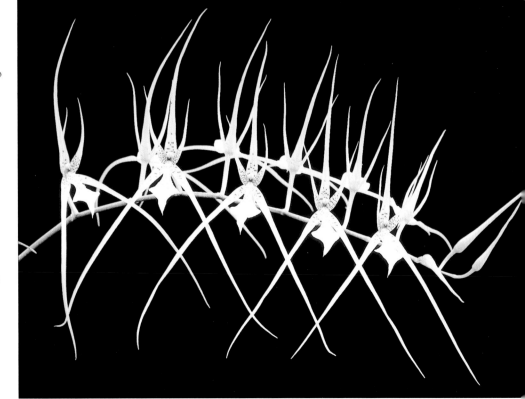

Grow any of these delectable orchid species in a cool greenhouse or indoors on a window-sill environment where they will receive good light all year, but not the direct sunlight in summer. Water, and feed lightly during the year, giving less of both in the winter to allow the plants to partially dry out in between waterings. The barkerias are the exception, and need to be kept quite dry while they are dormant and without leaves. In the spring these orchids will respond to the lengthening days with an explosion of new roots at the base of the new growth. Often these will skip over the pot surface altogether to remain truly aerial and become quite long. Encourage this fascinating feature by regular spraying of the roots. These orchids grow best in open slatted baskets, and can be suspended on a hook. They have very soft foliage and can be susceptible to attack from Red Spider Mite. When the leaves are shed in early winter, be sure to collect and burn them in case they are infected. Scale insects are the worst pest to attack the *Odontoglossum* family, and these should be watched out for during the summer. Should the foliage become yellowish, increase the shade and give extra feed.

Repot the barkerias annually before their roots commence and keep in as small a container as possible. Repot the remainder in this grouping every other year. The aspasias can be mounted on a bark slab if preferred.

These are all epiphytic orchids coming from South America.

226. *Barkeria spectabilis*. A species from Mexico and Guatemala which likes a distinct rest in winter when it is deciduous. The short stems are only 5cm high but produce large pink flowers. This orchid has a short but fast growing season when it can take in copious amounts of water and fertiliser.

Anguloas, lycastes and angulocastes

227. *Lycaste* David. A hybrid between *L. dowiana* and *L. cruenta*. Numerous flowers are produced from the base at the same time as the new growth. The showy blooms have a strong perfume.

The anguloas, lycastes and the bigeneric hybrid between the two, the *Angulocaste*, are a prominent group of mainly robust, large-growing plants best suited to greenhouse culture. Both species and hybrids are grown and there is such variety to be found within this group there is something for all tastes. Most specialist nurseries will have a range of plants to offer.

Anguloas, lycastes and angulocastes are deciduous or semi-deciduous sympodial orchids, producing strong, robust conical pseudobulbs with several large, plicate leaves during the spring and summer. Their roots are robust, brown and softly haired. When in full leaf these plants can be up to a metre tall, the foliage rising well above the flowers. They need plenty of space to spread their generous leaves which are an attractive feature and fascinating to watch as they develop. The various species can bloom at different seasons, but they peak in the spring, producing their flower spikes from the base of the leading pseudobulb, often in profusion. Each spike carries a single bloom which, in the lycastes, is typically three cornered. A triangle is formed by the sepals which are held out flat while the petals face forward cupped above the small lip. The erect *Anguloa* flowers, on the other hand are cupped, giving them their common name of Tulip Orchid. They are also called Cradle Orchids because they have a loosely hinged lip

partially hidden within the fleshy petals and sepals, which rocks when the flower is tipped. The best-known is *Anguloa clowesii* whose rich yellow, summer-produced blooms have a powerful fragrance. The angulocastes exhibit characteristics midway between the two genera, with large, semi-open blooms of a heavy, waxy texture. These can be 10cm or more across and come in a whole range of colours, from subtle creams and yellows to defiant strong reds and browns with other shades in between.

These noble orchids have a fast growing season and complete their pseudobulbs in record time. Intermediate type temperatures suit them best, with a minimum of 13°C–15°C, and a maximum of 30°C. The higher the temperature the higher should be the humidity to keep a balance. These orchids dislike combinations of hot and dry or cold and wet so avoid these extremes. When the new growths start in the spring, watering can commence with a light feed at alternate applications. As their growth speeds up, feed can be added to each watering until the completion of growth towards autumn, when it can be lessened to every other watering. As winter approaches some will lose all their foliage while others retain some leaves until the following spring. At this start to their resting time discontinue watering and give only an occasional wetting should the pseudobulbs become shrivelled.

Although a high humidity is beneficial during the summer, it is better not to spray the

228. *Anguloa clowesii.* Anguloas are related to lycastes and have a distinct growing and resting season. The flower spikes come from the new growth in spring producing wonderful, tulip-shaped blooms, with a tremendous perfume.

229. *Anguloa virginalis*. The growth habit and flowering season is the same as *A. clowesii*, but the pink flowers are a different shape. This beautiful orchid is well worth growing even though it is space consuming. Anguloas will readily interbreed with lycastes to produce angulocastes.

foliage which can quickly show signs of damp spots. Keep up the humidity by regular spraying of water around the plants and their surroundings. Their soft leaves will also require protection from the sun, and they will need considerable shade while in leaf. During the winter give these orchids all available light to ensure ripening and a good crop of flowers to come. The oldest pseudobulbs can be removed and used for propagating, but do not reduce their number to below four or five on the main plant as this may weaken it unnecessarily and decrease its flowering capabilities. It is far better to allow the plants to grow into big specimens where within a few years some may reach 30cm or more across. The growing of the largest plants in this family, the angulocastes, is not to be undertaken lightly!

This group are mainly epiphytic orchids spread throughout South America. They are also found growing terrestrially in the ground humus or upon moss-covered rocks as lithophytes.

230. *Lycaste deppei*. Now a rare species at one time common in Mexico and Guatemala. This is an attractive orchid to grow, which flowers freely in the spring.

231. *Bothrochilus bellus*. A pretty Mexican species producing clusters of flowers in great profusion around the base of the plant.

232. *Bollea coelestis*. This species comes from Colombia and is well-known for its large, fan-shaped array of foliage. The flower is a most unusual shade of mauve and blue. A well-grown plant will produce many flowers in the summer.

Bolleas, bothrochilus and cochleanthes

This grouping of three distinct genera have been placed together for convenience and to draw to attention the similarly-coloured species which can be found in each genus. A common factor is the blue-mauve colouring adorning at least three of the species, *Bollea lawrenceana*, *Bothrochilus bellus* and *Cochleanthes discolor*. These are connoisseurs' plants, from which virtually no hybridising has been done, and which are sometimes available through specialist nurseries.

Bolleas and cochleanthes produce leafy, fanned growths of narrowly oval leaves lacking pseudobulbs. Their roots are quite thick, white and fleshy. They are sympodial, evergreen plants of medium size. The flowers are produced singly on stems which do not rise above the foliage. The two species of *Bollea* most often seen are *B. lawrenceana* which has white, fleshy, welcoming flowers, the lip and lateral sepals tipped with magenta, while the larger, 6cm flowers of *Bollea coelestis* are closer to the elusive blue.

Cochleanthes, which has given rise to a number of intergeneric crosses with lesser-known members of its sub-tribe, is represented in specific collections by *C. discolor*, a dramatic species which has a large, projecting purple lip on the top of which lie the petals while the creamy-white, narrow sepals are held away from the flower.

Bothrochilus bellus produces hard, round pseudobulbs with long, narrow leaves. The

233. *Bollea lawrenceana.*
Closely related to *B. coelestis*, with which it will cross breed, this species is not as colourful, but has a much stronger perfume.

flower spikes cluster around the base each carrying several tube-like flowers which are white, their sepals tipped with magenta and the lip with yellow in a delightful combination of hues.

These orchids are at their best when grown warm and shady. An intermediate greenhouse where a temperature range from 13°C to 30°C, which varies with the seasons and day to day outdoor conditions, is perfect for them. They enjoy a high humidity when the temperature is high, but overhead spraying should be limited to warm sunny days when moisture on their soft leaves will dry out quickly. Water all year, but give less in the winter and allow the plants to partially dry out in between. Feed during the spring, summer and autumn months at about every third watering. These orchids prefer to be grown in pots, using a medium to fine grade of bark chippings. The growths and pseudobulbs should be left intact without dividing unless absolutely necessary. Older plants which have been left whole will sometimes fall apart under repotting, which is the safest method of division for these orchids.

These species all come from tropical American countries and are no longer imported from the wild. They are difficult and expensive to raise artificially and are thus rare in cultivation at this time.

234. *Cochleanthes discolor*. A lovely species to grow which quickly makes a specimen plant. It has a trumpet-shaped lip, bright colours and is a small, compact, easily accommodated orchid.

Bulbophyllums and cirrhopetalums

235. *Bulbophyllum graveolens*. This is a striking species with large displays of bright, golden-yellow flowers with red centres. The scent of these blooms is designed to attract carrion flies and is not at all pleasant.

The bulbophyllums form a huge genus of incredibly eccentric orchids with the cirrhopetalums not far behind. Among these two genera are some of the most weird and outrageous species, ranging from tiny plants with inconspicuous blooms to huge plants with grotesque, evil-smelling flowers. Yet, even among those with the least desirable attributes, there are devotees who would collect nothing else! Some of the more interesting varieties are occasionally available from specialist nurseries.

The plants have pseudobulbs of varying size and shapes spread out along a creeping rhizome, with an oval leaf. Their roots are often scant and short, the flowers may be born singly or numerously clustered on the stem. The cirrhopetalums bear their flowers at the end of the stem in an umbel, often with incredible results. The blooms of bulbophyllums are amazingly variable, posing the question as to how they can all be members of the same genus. It is therefore impossible to describe the typical *Bulbophyllum*, but if it has strange-looking, bad-smelling flowers with the ability to hold you in with an unerring fascination, it is probably a *Bulbophyllum*. Equally evocative are the cirrhopetalums, which can be quite stunning on a large plant dripping with flowers. The long, tapering sepals of some species are quite unlike anything else among the orchids, and form the main attraction. The petals and lip are diminutive and partially hidden at the centre of the bloom. A number of the bulbophyllums have similar flowers while others are different again. An extreme example is *Bulbophyllum falcatum*, which produces a flattened stem along which the small beetle-like flowers appear at regular

236. *Bulbophyllum lobbii*. This amazing looking orchid has a freely moving lip that allows an alighting insect to gain access to the pollinia.

237. *Bulbophyllum* Jersey. A colourful hybrid from *B. lobbii* x *B. echinolabium*. It will easily grow into a specimen plant producing many startling blooms.

238. *Bulbophyllum falcatum*. One of the most unusual species to come from Africa, with flower spikes which grow at right angles to the plant.

239 (Opposite). *Cirrhopetalum* Elizabeth Ann 'Bucklebury' AM/RHS. Probably the most well-known *Cirrhopetalum* hybrid, grown throughout the world for its fascinating, unusually shaped flowers.

intervals. *B. lobbii* is more dramatic and has a hinged rocking lip which slams its pollinator onto the pollinia, while *B.careyanum* is the nearest any orchid comes to resemble a dog dropping. The least attractive the flower is to our eyes, the worse the smell. Many have no scent at all.

The smaller of these orchids will grow happily mounted, or in baskets where they can be suspended, and in this way a plant can remain in the same container until it has completely encircled it, growing into a solid ball. Most are easily divideable until they become large. The smaller-growing species will require a finer grade of bark.

The two genera produce sympodial, evergreen plants which will grow well indoors or in a cool to intermediate greenhouse. When purchasing plants for a greenhouse, be sure to enquire which section your chosen specimen has been growing in. Otherwise, a temperature range of 13°C to 30°C will suit most varieties.

During all but the winter months these orchids can be watered and sprayed regularly, with some light feed added at every third watering. During the winter reduce the watering giving just enough to maintain plump pseudobulbs, and discontinue feed until the spring. Full light is necessary in the winter for the plants to bloom well, which they may do at almost any time. Some species will give several flowerings throughout the year, while others have a more definite regime. While their colouring may be more sombre than bright, the impact of some species is nothing less then startling.

While most of the 1,000 or so species of bulbophyllums and cirrhopetalums combined inhabit South East Asia, they have spread throughout the world to Africa, Australia, and South America, which goes some way to explaining their huge diversity. All are epiphytic, the plants growing to massive proportions sometimes encircling whole branches or tree trunks of trees.

240. *Bulbophyllum falcatum*. A close-up showing the flattened stem and the rows of small, insect-like flowers.

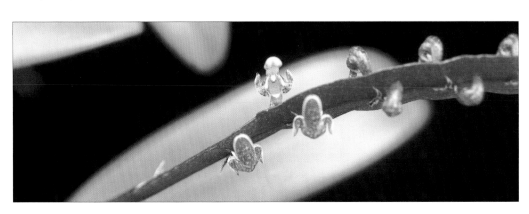

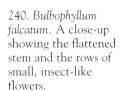

241. *Bifrenaria tyrianthina*. A species from Brazil bearing one to three highly-coloured flowers on a flower spike. This small, compact growing plant is well worth growing in the cool greenhouse or in the home.

242 (Below). *Dendrochilum arachnites*, showing the flowers in close-up.

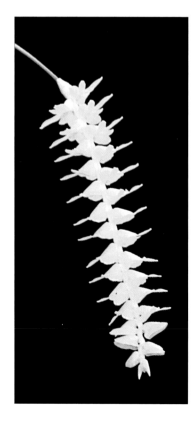

Bifrenarias and dendrochilums

Two completely different genera are linked here as 'stable companions'. Both produce plants of similar size and require the same growing conditions being easily cultivated indoors or in a cool greenhouse. Both are ideal beginners' orchids but with a difference. In each genus just two or three species are in cultivation, with no hybrids. Plants which are occasionally available from the specialist nurseries, will be nursery raised propagations or divisions of larger stock.

Bifrenarias produce yellowish, four-cornered, cone-shaped pseudobulbs with a single rigid, dark green, broadly oval leaf. Their roots are quite thick and abundant. Dendrochilums have smaller, oval-shaped pseudobulbs which support a single, narrow leaf, and have a fine root system. If there are similar characteristics in their plant structure, in their flowers these two companions could not be more different. The bifrenarias flower from the base of the leading pseudobulbs on short spikes which bear one to two large, 5cm wide flowers which have broad, waxy petals and sepals, creamy white to pink with a hairy mauve lip. The more colourful of the popular species is *Bifrenaria tyrianthina*, whose soft, compelling beauty is enhanced by its fragrance.

Dendrochilums are resplendent in the common name of Silver Chain Orchids. Their flower spikes are produced from the new growths before they have matured, and are extremely thin and wiry. Under the weight of their numerous, small, and tightly packed delicate flowers, they quickly assume an attractive drooping habit. These neat little flowers can be white, as in *Dendrochilum cobbianum*, which has a very powerful vanilla-like scent, or golden-yellow as in *D. arachnites*, whose shorter chains of delightful, spiky little flowers could be mistaken for caterpillars. If you should be fortunate enough to acquire one of these species, guard it well and grow it on into a specimen plant, when you will be amply rewarded with a display which is second to none. These two very different orchids will bloom during the early summer months filling the air with their scent for up to three weeks.

Grow these orchids in a cool situation where the temperatures can range throughout the year from 10°C to 30°C. Probably the more important of these temperatures is the winter night time, when if kept too warm they may be reluctant to bloom. Water the plants all year, but give much less in the winter, allowing them the opportunity of drying out in between waterings. Feed can be applied at every third watering during the rest of the year. The plants do best in pots, and can be repotted every other year but take care not to overpot. Both types will grow quickly into specimen plants which makes them so rewarding.

243. *Dendrochilum arachnites*. One of the rarer dendrochilums, seldom seen in cultivation, originating from the Philippines, and flowering in early summer.

They are not particularly bothered by any specific greenhouse insects and, where good growing conditions prevail, the usual pests should not get a hold. The plants are evergreen, and usually lose the occasional leaf from time to time. If a rapid leaf-loss should occur, the problem will undoubtedly be with the roots. Remove the plant from its pot and if the roots are found to be dead it is most probably through overwatering. It may be necessary to divide the plant into smaller portions and pot each into as small a container as possible with fresh bark compost to which a quantity of chopped *Sphagnum* moss has been added.

These two distinct genera grow epiphytically in forest areas. The bifrenarias come from the New World, inhabiting Trinidad and Panama down to parts of Brazil. The dendrochilums are Old World orchids, originating from Indonesia to New Guinea and the Philippines.

244 (Above). *Dendrochilum cobbianum*. A species with dense sprays of small, highly-fragrant flowers. Its compact habit makes it well worth including in any collection.

245. *Dendrochilum cobbianum*. A close-up of the flowers, showing the detail.

246 (Opposite). *Liparis nutans*. This species has very attractive flowers with round, reddish-brown lips. Many flower spikes are produced on a small, compact plant.

247 (Right). *Liparis nutans*. A close-up of the flower showing the intricate petal formation and pure white column which carries the pollinia.

Disas, liparis and malaxis

Here is a trio of unrelated orchids which illustrate extreme diversity. They are just three examples randomly picked from among thousands of fascinating plants you can grow. All are of a convenient size and have much to offer the enthusiast, but there the similarity ends. Look out for these and similar little jewels at the specialist nurseries.

Disas are terrestrial orchids which produce a rosette of soft, narrow leaves in the spring. As the plant develops a flower spike extends from the centre and opens with several distinctly unique flowers. While all species are colourful and varied, the most popular to gain favour is *Disa uniflora*. This one species, and several very fine hybrids which have been raised from it, of which *D. Diores* is an example, has carried the genus into a prominent position in collections. The flowers are typically triangular, the shape arising from the splendidly vibrant rich-red and orange sepals. The lip and petals are much reduced, and hardly visible at the centre of the bloom. The glistening flowers are intricately veined with crimson and are among the brightest of all orchid blooms. After flowering the plants die down to become dormant for the winter. During this stage the plants are left cool and dry until the new growth is seen in the early spring. These are high altitude plants from Table Mountain in South Africa, and need to be grown extremely cool to succeed. A winter temperature just a few degrees above freezing is adequate and cool summer days are also necessary. Although these plants can be difficult for the beginner to cope with, where their more specialised requirements are met, the rewards are many. Repot annually into a house plant-type of compost.

248 (Left). *Liparis lyonii*. The delicate miniature flowers are highly collectable species for growers who seek the unusual. Most of the *Liparis* come from the Far East.

249. *Disa* Diores 'Inca Warrior'. The disas are a fascinating genus from South Africa. Only a few have been used for hybridisation which produces fantastic flame-red flowers.

Liparis are a genus of very mixed species, which come from the world over. They appear equally at home in the tropics as well as in temperate regions of the northern hemisphere. Most are terrestrial but some of the species from India and South East Asia are epiphytes. *Liparis lyonii* is typical of this latter group, the plants having diminutive pseudobulbs at the base of the stout leaves. All produce similar looking flowers, which are tiny, often densely packed on the upright stem, and which need the assistance of a magnifying glass to be seen in detail. This will reveal intricate, insect-like flowers with large lips. In Europe, *L. loeselii* or Fen Orchid produces plants just a few centimetres high.

Related to *Liparis* is *Malaxis*, another genus which is distributed widely throughout the world, with both terrestrial and epiphytic species occurring. One example is *Malaxis latifolia*, which is a pretty terrestrial species with lovely lush foliage produced from pseudobulbs during the summer. The flower spikes emerge from the centre of the leaves and are packed with minute, reddish flowers. The unopened buds remain light green, giving the stem a two-tone effect. Both *Liparis* and *Malaxis* are cool-growing orchids, which need a decided rest during the winter when their pots can be allowed to dry out. During the summer they need shady conditions indoors or in a cool greenhouse where there is not too much humidity, which can spot their soft foliage. Repot annually and grow in a compost of fine bark chippings, or house-plant compost. Feed lightly during the months while the plants are active. The tiny, captivating flowers are all produced during the summer months.

250 (Left). *Malaxis latifolia* 'Frisky'. One of the prettiest in the genus with extremely small flowers produced in succession on upright flower spikes. The yellow buds open dark red.

251 (Below). *Malaxis latifolia* 'Frisky'. A close-up shows how the blooms are formed around the flower spike.

Masdevallias and related genera

252. *Dryadella zebrina.*
A true miniature orchid, easily accommodated in any cool house collection. The unusual flowers, nestling at the base of the plant, produce a very strong scent.

Should you develop a liking for the smaller growing and flowered orchids, there is a host of species in several genera which come under the umbrella of one sub family. They are never-ending in their diversity and all are fascinating subjects which, like good wine, are an acquired taste. Every one is worth taking a close look at, for among these tiny jewels are some of the most surprising gems in the orchid family. Among these plants, small is definitely beautiful! The following, and similar species will be found in the specialist nurseries.

Masdevallias produce tufted growth, the smallest a few centimetres high to the largest at about 15cm. Their root system is very fine, and they need to be grown in as small a container as possible. Open netted basket-pots suit them well. Their flowers are three cornered, the large sepals sometimes adorned with long tails, and tiny petals and lip at the centre of the bloom. This appearance has earned them their common name of Kite Orchids. Some species, and a number of excellent hybrids, are extremely colourful. Their flowers are produced at various times during the year, peaking during the spring and summer. Closely related to the masdevallias are the dryadellas. These are small growing plants, with tufted foliage and flowers which nestle low down. *Dryadella zebrina* is one of several species known affectionately as 'Pheasants-in-the-grass', for the half-hidden, brown spotted flowers which crouch down among the leaves. Often, they are smelt before they are seen! There is no trouble seeing the flowers of *Physosiphon tubatus* however. This species carries its blooms aloft on slender spikes above the foliage. The

253. *Masdevallia* Inca Prince. There are many *Masdevallia* hybrids today, all of which produce these unique, highly coloured three-cornered flowers. They are easily accommodated in a small pot.

254. *Masdevallia molossus*. One of the more botanical species of this genus which will intrigue the collector of the unusual. It is a cool growing plant from South America.

individual, buff-yellow, semi-opening tubed flowers all face one way on the stem. A similar arrangement of flowers on slender stems is produced by the stelis. There are numerous species within this genus which are extremely difficult to identify, they are so alike. A hand-lens will reveal large sepals and minute petals and lip in perfect detail. Even more amazing are the minute flowers of *Platystele*. In the species *Platystele misera*, tiny ruddy flowers appear to chase each other along the stem in a race to reach the top. Decidedly insect-like are the flowers of *Restrepia*, of which *R. langsbergii* is typical. The lateral sepals have become fused to form a large, inviting platform for the pollinating insect which is welcomed literally, with open arms, in the form of projecting narrow petals. This genus produces a succession of these exquisite blooms over a very long period from stems at the base of each leaf.

These species are all cool growing orchids which can be accommodated indoors or in a cool greenhouse. Being so small, they are ideal subjects for an indoor growing case, which may be a fish tank or aquarium used for reptiles. Because of their small size, it can

255 (Above). *Physosiphon tubatus*. One of the small, many-flowered species that quickly grow into specimen plants. This little plant is popular with growers of masdevallias and other small species.

256 (Left). *Physosiphon tubatus*. This shows a close-up of the three-petalled flowers, of a plant easily accommodated in the small greenhouse.

257 (Opposite). *Stelis aprica*. This genus is best grown with masdevallias and pleurothallis. Although the blooms are extremely small, large quantities are freely produced on numerous flower spikes, making them a compact and attractive species to grow.

258. *Platystele misera*. Although this plant is not the smallest in the genus, the flowers are extremely delicate, borne on cotton-thin stems.

259 (Left). *Platystele misera*. A close-up of the individual blooms showing the crystalline patterning on the petals, and the bright red lip.

be extremely difficult to keep these little plants evenly moist throughout the year, without the extremes of their becoming too dry or too wet at any time. By keeping them in an enclosed environment, provided there is plenty of air from an open top, they can do very much better with their own micro-climate. In the base of the tank place small pebbles which can be kept moist, and stand the tiny orchids on small upturned pots. A bell jar will also make a suitable home for a few of these little plants which will reward with copious blooms throughout the year.

All these orchids come from South and Central America where the smallest are twig epiphytes, growing on the extremities of branches and growing into good sized cushions.

260. *Restrepia sanguinea*. This is a species from Colombia in South America. The flower is twice the size of *R. langsbergii*. Restrepias will often flower several times from old flower spikes so these should not be removed until completely withered.

261. *Restrepia langsbergii*. The restrepias are a small genus of orchids which grow well with masdevallias in the cool house with a minimum winter night temperature of 10°C.

Oncidiums, cyrtochilums and rossioglossums

262 (Above). *Oncidium sphacelatum*. This has been used extensively for hybridising long stemmed oncidiums. This plant will stand a wide range of temperatures and flower freely in most parts of the world.

A trio of highly colourful orchids which are related to the odontoglossums mentioned earlier. The oncidiums are a large genus of which a number of species, and fewer hybrids, are available. Most of the hybrids are intergeneric crosses made with odontoglossums. Of the closely-related cyrtochilums only a very few species and occasional hybrid are in cultivation, these mostly the province of the collector. Rossioglossums are similarly rare in cultivation, with just one or two species and hybrids occasionally seen, and available from the specialist nurseries.

Oncidiums are highly variable plants, varying in size from 10cm to 45cm tall. They produce green, oval pseudobulbs with a pair of narrow, light green leaves. Their roots are extremely fine and can become very long where plants are mounted. Those species which produce their pseudobulbs along a creeping rhizome are best grown in this way. Others do well in pot culture. Typically the flowers are yellow, although pink is also well represented in the genus. Often these are large lipped, bright yellow platforms dominating the smaller sepals and petals which are mostly yellow and spotted with

263 (Opposite). *Oncidium* Boissiense. This is pure breeding produced mainly from *Oncidium varicosum* giving these bright golden yellow lips.

264. *Oncidium maculatum*. A warm, tolerant *Oncidium* which will breed with odontoglossums. Sometimes scented, depending on the species. It makes a very interesting parent.

265. *Oncidium longipes*. One of the miniature oncidiums, easily contained in a small flower pot, which produces several flower spikes with two to three flowers per spike.

266. *Cyrtochilum macranthum* x *chrysodypterum*. This is a high altitude Colombian *Cyrtochilum*. The flower spikes can be anything up to ten or twelve feet long and are therefore wound round in a continuous hoop in cultivation to make them more easily accommodated.

brown as in the hybrid *Oncidium* Boissiense, where the flowers are carried on side branches to the main spike. *Oncidium maculatum* represents a distinct group whose flowers are more symmetrical, with other colour combinations.

The cyrtochilums have similar looking but more robust plants. They produce their flowers at intervals along an extremely long flower-spike which may extend to 4 metres. In their natural habitat these flower spikes drape over branches in a vine-like way, but in cultivation they are most easily handled by winding them in a circle between two canes. The flowers are attractive and long lasting. *Cyrtochilum macranthum* x *chrysodypterum* is one of only a handful of hybrids which have been made in this group.

The rossioglossums are a very small genus of extraordinarily good-looking flowers. The showiest is *Rossioglossum grande* and its hybrid *R*. Rawdon Jester. These produce huge,

267. *Rossioglossum* Rawdon Jester. A close up of the centre of the flower, showing the characteristic little figure in the centre of the lip, giving this orchid its common name of Clown Orchid.

8cm–10cm wide flowers which are highly glossed in rich chestnut and yellow, the shell-shaped lip semi-circled with red brown. At the centre of the bloom sits the replica of a small clown, clearly giving this orchid its common name of Clown Orchid.

The above are mainly cool growing orchids, although among the oncidiums are some which prefer warmer conditions. For the cool varieties a temperature range of between 10°C and 30°C is ideal. They enjoy good light, and most do well when placed out of doors for the summer. Winter care should involve good light with sufficient watering to prevent shrivelling of the pseudobulbs. The rossioglossums prefer a dryer winter rest. They commence their new growth late in the spring, and bloom shortly after while this is still young. Their foliage is an attractive dark green, the undersides of the leaves peppered with darker colouring. This shows up well on the new growths. Light feeding at every third watering is sufficient during the spring, summer and autumn when the plants are most active. The more robust of the species can be propagated by removing any surplus pseudobulbs during repotting. Some of the oncidiums, such as *Oncidium flexuosum* produce their pseudobulbs along an upward creeping rhizome, and these are better suited to growing on a mount where their long aerial roots will grow downward to form a thick mat which becomes a feature of the plant.

These are South and Central American epiphytic plants which are popular with growers throughout the world.

268 (Opposite). *Rossioglossum* Rawdon Jester. A hybrid between *R. grande* and *R. williamsianum*, these beautiful and long-lasting blooms will survive in a dry atmosphere, making this plant excellent for a cool room. Both species originate from Guatemala.

Orchis, ophrys, platantheras and dactylorhizas

Terrestrial orchids abound the world over. Mostly they are less conspicuous than the showiest of the epiphytes, but growing in dense colonies containing thousands of plants they can be quite stunning. They have not inspired the imagination in the same way as the epiphytes having proved less easy to grow. In recent years, however, modern propagation methods have produced strong, artificially bred plants which are suitable for garden cultivation or a frost-free alpine glasshouse. Some varieties are obtainable from hardy-plant nurseries and bulb merchants. Most types, however, are best left in their natural habitats where they still exist, including the strangest of all which come from the grasslands and plains of South Australia. These highly specialised species are beyond the scope of this book. The following will give a little insight into a few of the plants which can still be found growing wild in many areas.

Orchis produce exotic-looking foliage with fleshy, dark green, purple blotched leaves which form a basal rosette and from the centre of which the flower spike emerges in early summer. The flowers of O. mascula are rich mauve, although its common name is Early Purple Orchid. They are strong smelling, with a fat spur behind the lip. After flowering, the seed capsules form and the plant dies down for the winter. *Orchis mascula* inhabits most of Europe and is also known in western Asia and North Africa. It is often

269 (Above). *Orchis mascula* (Early Purple Orchid) is a great opportunist, quick to colonise any piece of wasteland. It grows wild and is abundant in most parts of Europe. Seen here flowering on a roadside verge in England in May.

270 (Left). *Ophrys apifera*. The Bee Orchid, growing in long grass. This plant is liable to show many variations depending on the part of the country where it naturally occurs and blooms in May or June.

271. *Platanthera bifolia*. The Lesser Butterfly Orchid grows wild in Europe in undisturbed pastures. It flowers in mid-summer with tall spikes which will vary in length depending on the surrounding foliage and can be anything up to 60cm high.

one of the first plants to colonise newly disturbed ground. Evidence of this can be found along motorway verges where the plants build up into large colonies, their tall purple spires adding grace and colour from early May.

Ophrys are distinguished by their large, fleshy lips which in some species resemble the body of an insect, a spider, or fly, whichever creature pollinates the flower. They are mainly small growing, and take some searching out in long grasses. Two broad leaves are produced by the *Platanthera* species from which arises the stem, which carries numerous creamy-white flowers with long spurs. The extended petals gives *P. chlorantha* the name Greater Butterfly Orchid.

While it is illegal to dig up the plants, or even pick the flowers of these British native orchids, many of which are extremely rare, those mentioned above are worth looking for at specialist nurseries. These can be grown in pots or pans using a leaf-mould compost to which fine grit has been added for good drainage. Out of doors where the climate is suitable, you can make up a bed of good humus for these to grow. Left undisturbed they will form good sized colonies.

272. *Phragmipedium besseae.* An exciting new discovery found in the Andes in the early 1980s this species has created a revolution in *Phragmipedium* breeding, and is responsible for all the new red-orange hybrids.

Phragmipediums

The discovery in 1981 of an incredible, richly coloured, previously unknown species *Phragmipedium besseae*, has shot this once underrated genus to prominence. These large-growing, mainly terrestrial, evergreen Slipper Orchids now claim a revival of interest resulting in a massive hybridising programme which has created some of the most colourful varieties available from the specialist nurseries. The species have the characteristic pouch which defines all the Slipper Orchids, and a number of these have extremely long, ribbon-like petals. In some species (*P. caudatum*), the petals reach down for over 30cm. These plants have long been rare in cultivation, with a few hybrids improving upon the species. The appearance of *P. besseae* has created a whole new range of flame-coloured hybrids, which are now more easily available and which have surpassed the species for popularity.

The plants produce strong growths consisting of several long, strap-like leaves. Their roots are numerous and brown, similar to the paphiopedilums. The flower spikes, which can become quite tall and produce a succession of flowers, come from the centre of the latest mature growth. Plants which are 50cm to 60cm tall, can produce flower spikes over one metre high. They grow best in a greenhouse where there is sufficient headroom for their large bulk.

273 (Opposite). *Phragmipedium longifolium.* This species has been in cultivation for many years. As each old flower drops, a new bud will quickly open on the same stem. On a large mature plant, the stem is capable of blooming continuously for eighteen months.

274. *Phragmipedium* China Dragon is one of the latest and most impressive of the hybrids raised from *P. besseae*. In this case crossed with *P. grande*, the long petals of the latter and the bright colouring from the former are combined.

275 (Opposite). *Phragmipedium* Sorceror's Apprentice. A hybrid from the species *Phragmipedium longifolium* with fascinating, twisted petals. The picture shows clearly the succession of buds waiting to open.

276 (Right). *Phragmipedium* Don Wimber. This is an example of what is being achieved by using *Phragmipedium besseae* as a parent. These large, long lasting, beautiful flowers are produced in succession.

277 (Below). *Phragmipedium* Grouville. This is another exciting modern hybrid which has been produced from *Phragmipedium besseae*, to bring out the flaming red and orange colouring.

278 (Opposite). *Phragmipedium* Living Fire. This new, red-flowered variety shows a new shape of flower produced on a long stem.

Phragmipediums need intermediate conditions, with a minimum winter night temperature of 12°C to 15°C, rising during the day to a maximum of 30°C in summer. They enjoy shady conditions in a humid atmosphere, but can be given more light in the winter. Avoid getting the plants too wet or their surroundings too damp when the temperature is low. Water all year, and apply feed at every other watering during the growing season, with reduced feeding during the winter months. These orchids do not have a resting period, but will slow their growth in accordance with the shorter days and

low light of winter. Phragmipediums will grow well in a coarse bark compost, or the inert equivalent of Rockwool. This latter ensures that they can be kept evenly moist at the roots without the danger of overwatering. Where good growing conditions prevail, Red Spider Mite, which can otherwise attack the undersides of the foliage on these orchids, will be kept at bay.

The species originate from South America, often growing out of crevices in limestone rocks or cliff faces, in inaccessible places.

Pleiones, thunias and calanthes

This grouping of three unrelated genera are combined for their horticultural similarities. All are deciduous and need to be kept completely dry for the winter, to the extent of removing them from their pots and lying the dormant pseudobulbs or stems in trays. Pleiones are easily obtained from multiple stores and nurseries. Thunias and calanthes are seen less often and are available from specialist nurseries. Pleione species and various hybrids are available. Among the thunias, one or two lovely species are grown, with very little hybridising having been done. Very few *Calanthe* species are available and only a few more hybrids.

Pleiones produce small, squat pseudobulbs which live for just two years, and retain their single, ribbed leaf for one season only. The single flower, 6cm to 8cm across, and large for the size of plant, is produced from the centre of the new growth in early spring, and lasts for a period of ten days. Numerous pseudobulbs can be planted in a large pan to create a gorgeous show. Their colours range through snow-white to delicate shell-pink and stronger mauves with the occasional yellow.

Thunias produce rigid, cane-like stems which start their development in early spring and grow at a fast pace throughout the summer to terminate in a flower spike of frothy, tumbling blooms, each 10cm across. These are glistening white with a colourful, hairy lip. This is about the only orchid which displays autumn colours, all its leaves turning from green to yellow, gold and brown before falling, to leave the bare, silvery canes.

The deciduous calanthes produce firm, silvery pseudobulbs which support a number of papery, wide ribbed leaves. These remain all summer while the pseudobulb is growing and are shed in early winter as the flower spike appears at the base. The upright, hairy flower spike produces a dense cascade of attractive flowers, which range from white with red lips to pink and deep red. Once these orchids were firm favourites of the Victorian growers who prized them for table decorations during the winter festive season. These deciduous calanthes are distinct from the evergreen species which come from China and Japan, and which are not so widely grown as they deserve to be.

Grow pleiones in a very cool situation where they will not suffer from overheating while they are active. An outside cold-frame, or north facing window-sill will suit them. Black tips to the leaves during their growing season may indicate temperatures which are too warm. During the winter they need a dry rest in good light in a cool frost-free position. Water and feed well when they are potted up, but keep the soft foliage dry. Repot annually before flowering using a fine bark or house-plant compost for these mainly terrestrial orchids. Take care not to bury the pseudobulbs which should sit on the surface. As the new roots are produced they will become firm in their pot.

279 (Opposite). *Pleione formosana.* This is the easiest of the pleiones to grow, and is a highly variable species. Here are dark pink to pure white clones.

   Grow thunias and calanthes in a warm room indoors or the intermediate section of
the greenhouse where they can be given plenty of water and feed while they are
growing, but keep the leaves dry to avoid spotting. The thunias will require potting up
when the new growths start to show at the base. Support the leafless stem by tying to a
bamboo cane which is potted up with it, leaving the new growths to sit on the surface.
Calanthes need to be potted up in a similar way, using a bark-based compost or

280. *Pleione* Shantung 'Ridgeway' AM/RHS. This is one of the finest of the hybrids which produces large, robust pseudobulbs and beautiful, soft-peach flowers.

Rockwool. Keep these plants well shaded in summer and remove to a high shelf where there is good winter light after they have been removed from their pots at the start of winter, or after flowering.

Pleiones originate from China and Formosa as well as ports of south east Asia. Thunias are terrestrial orchids coming mainly from India, but also occurring in China and parts of south east Asia. Calanthes come mainly from Thailand and parts of Asia. Those in cultivation have been propagated for many years to retain an ongoing stock.

281 (Opposite). *Thunia* Gattonensis (*T. marjorensis* x *T. winniana*). The most beautiful of the thunias producing large heads of frothy blooms in late summer. This hybrid was originally raised many years ago, and little or no breeding has been done within this group since.

282. *Stanhopea graveolens*. A very beautiful species with large flowers which comes from central South America.

Stanhopeas, Gongoras and Neomoorea

Stanhopeas and gongoras are related genera which produce some of the most extraordinary of orchid flowers. They can be described as weird, outlandish or handsomely ugly! *Neomoorea* is a monotypic genus, which means that it contains a solitary species, *N. irrorata.* This is rare in cultivation and holds a certain fascination for anyone who is lucky enough to see it flower and observe the perfect butterfly-shaped lip. Several amazing strongly scented *Stanhopea* species are grown and a few hybrids are occasionally available from specialist nurseries. The *Gongora* species were once more plentiful than today. They have become scarce through importing restrictions and have

283 (Opposite). *Neomoorea irrorata*. This is a giant species making huge pseudobulbs the size of coconuts with long, heavy leaves. It is the only species in the genus. The beautiful flowers have a tiny lip resembling a small butterfly. It comes from Panama and is best grown in the warm house.

284. *Stanhopea grandiflora*. One of the more unusual and less cultivated of the species, it has a beautiful creamy-white tone to the flowers and a strong pleasing perfume.

a limited appeal for their highly scented, oddly-formed flowers, which are occasionally available from specialist nurseries.

Stanhopeas and gongoras produce cone-shaped to rounded, ribbed pseudobulbs. The stanhopeas carry a single semi-rigid, wide, ribbed leaf, and the gongoras, which are somewhat smaller, carry a pair of oval leaves. *Neomoorea irrorata* produces very large, rounded pseudobulbs and correspondingly large and ribbed leaves. The flower spike which comes from the base of the latest pseudobulb reaches below the foliage. Stanhopeas and gongoras are unusual for their downward flower spikes which, in stanhopeas, will burrow through the compost to emerge underneath the plant in its basket. *Gongora* flower spikes grow horizontally to the edge of the container pouring their flowers over the rim. Their main colouring is through light browns and yellows, often spotted on their petals and sepals.

285. *Stanhopea oculata*. This species probably bears the largest number of flowers in the genus. A large, spreading flower spike hangs beneath the plant, reminiscent of a chandelier.

Stanhopea flowers are large and very fleshy. Most species, such as the red-spotted *S. tigrina*, have two horn-like projections on either side of the lip which assist the pollinating insect. The petals and sepals are thrown back away from the lip to reveal clearly this part of the flower. The high colouring of this species and strong scent ensures early pollination of these flowers which last three to four days. Large plants will produce a succession of flower spikes opening over a period which greatly extends the summer flowering season.

These orchids are all cool to intermediate growers. Ideally, they like greenhouse conditions where there is a temperature range of from 12°C to 30°C. They need partial shade in summer and full light in winter. Water *N. irrorata* and gongoras well in summer and give less in winter while they are resting. Stanhopeas often grow during the winter and rest in the summer, so need the reverse in their watering and feeding regime.

286. *Stanhopea nigroviolacea.* Showing the large buds just prior to opening. These usually open at dawn, often with a loud pop.

287. *Stanhopea nigroviolacea.* This is the largest-flowered of the stanhopeas and it emits a powerful perfume. Sadly, it only lasts a few days in perfection.

288. *Gongora truncata*
A species best grown in a basket and hung up in the greenhouse where numerous, pendent spikes produce strangely enchanting flowers. This is a species from central South America.

The plants can be overhead sprayed during the summer, when they enjoy good humidity. Grow in hanging baskets and repot every other year or so. Always at their best when grown into large specimens where room permits, they can be divided when necessary and grown on from surplus back bulbs. The *Neomoorea* needs to be grown in a large pot sufficient for its size.

These are all South and Central American species, growing as epiphytes on large trees, and often producing short, spiky aerial roots, which grow upwards from the base of the plant and become hard and rigid when mature. These needle-sharp roots form a protective barrier around the base of the plant.

289. *Maxillaria ochroleuca*. A small growing, compact species with wispy, spidery flowers which are short-lived, highly scented and numerous.

290. *Zygopetalum crinitum*. One of the most compact growing zygopetalums, this species produces strongly-scented, long-lasting flowers.

Maxillarias and zygopetalums

Among these two genera are found several interesting and varied species, a number of which find much favour with indoor growers. The smaller plants among the maxillarias are truly delightful, often well scented, and bloom profusely during their season. Their ease of growing contributes to their demand by beginners to this exotic hobby. There are very few hybrids to add to an extensive range of colourful species. The zygopetalums are a genus containing fewer species, the most popular in cultivation include *Zygopetalum mackayi* and *Z. crinitum*. These species typify the genus with their striking green and brown flowers dominated by a large, flared, indigo-stained lip. These species are also fragrant. A selection of these orchids will be found in most of the specialist nurseries.

Maxillarias vary enormously in size. All produce pseudobulbs which support a single leaf and often have basal leaf bracts which harden with age. Mostly the single flowers are produced on short to very short flower spikes. Among the largest flowered is *Maxillaria grandiflora* which produces large, red-spotted, white flowers around the base.

291. *Maxillaria triloris.*
A free-flowering
species producing a
regiment of boldly
marked blooms around
the base.

These are typically three-corned, with large sepals and smaller petals and lip. Among the smallest of the popular varieties M. *ochroleuca* is one of the showiest, producing a profusion of spidery yellow flowers with a pleasant fragrance. Other varieties have very dark, almost black flowers, but these belong in the collections of specialist growers.

Zygopetalums are robust plants with rounded pseudobulbs and several long and narrow leaves. The flower spikes come from the base of the new growth while it is partially developed, and the large blooms last for several weeks during the early summer. The plants can become fairly large, and need plenty of headroom for their flowers which reach above the foliage on some species.

These orchids are cool growing, many of the smaller maxillarias are ideal for indoor culture, while the larger-growing plants and the zygopetalums are more suited to a greenhouse. They enjoy cool, shady and moist conditions during the summer, when the

292. *Maxillaria grandiflora*. One of the largest of the maxillarias producing huge, grand looking flowers nestling amongst the foliage. A species from the Andes.

temperature should not go above 30°C in the day. A drop to 10°C at night during the winter is sufficient for them. During the winter give less water, but keep the plants evenly moist during the summer when feed can be added at every third watering. Scale insects and Red Spider Mite will attack these orchids and need to be watched for, particularly when temperatures are high in summer. Grow in pots and repot every other year, using a fine grade of bark for the smaller maxillarias and a coarser bark or Rockwool for the larger species of *Maxillaria* and *Zygopetalum*.

Maxillarias belong to a large genus with species coming from all over tropical America where they grow mainly as epiphytes. Zygopetalums also originate from South America, being found as far down as Argentina. They grow as terrestrials or epiphytes, their strong fleshy roots often travelling far absorbing moisture and nutrients from the debris which collects in the fork of branches.

Index

Page numbers in **bold** type refer to illustrations and captions